Reversal

William G. Kurtz, Jr.

William Kurtz
February 2016

ISBN: 978-1-946978-05-9

Disclaimer

This book is intended for educational purposes only. The author makes no warranty, whether express or implied, of future investing or trading profits as a result of use of this book, or otherwise; nor does the author make any warranty, whether express or implied, that the patterns which are described in this book will work as described, or at all; or that the eventual outcome of pattern processes which may now be in motion at the time of this writing will come to an end in any particular manner. Every investor makes his or her own investment decisions, and is solely responsible for them. PAST PERFORMANCE IS NO GUARANTEE OF FUTURE RESULTS.

Dedication

This book is dedicated to my beautiful wife, Patricia, who puts up with my faults and foibles without complaint.

I also dedicate it to my son Paul, who really knows his way around "Japanese Candlesticks" and the nooks and crannies of "Candelaabra," and was a great help to me in the layout of the book; and to my grandson Dan, who designed the Cover Page and the Back Page.

Acknowledgment

I wish to acknowledge the gracious cooperation of Genesis Financial Technologies, Inc., the owner of Trade Navigator©, by whose consent Trade Navigator© charts appear throughout this book.

Table of Contents

Prologue

Candelaabra® - What Is It?

"Candelaabra"® is a technical analysis system for use in all time frames in all charted financial markets – stocks, stock Indexes, the metals, all of the other Commodities, Bonds, and Forex. It works exactly the same in all of them, in all time frames. The primary advantage of "Candelaabra" is its uncanny ability to ferret out Reversals of Trend very early – even before the Reversal pattern has fully formed. It is not, therefore, a trend-*following* system; rather, it is a trend-*identification* system. We want to catch Reversals of Trend early – either to jump aboard a new trend as it is forming, or to enable us to get out of an existing position when the trend goes against us, before much damage has been done.

The whole purpose of Candelaabra® is to identify incipient trend reversals very early.

"Candelaabra" uses the "Japanese Candlesticks" style of financial price presentation as its base. "Candelaabra" goes on from there to include elements of "Elliott Wave;" but most especially it incorporates my discoveries that:

(1) *Contemporaneous extreme readings* in Price and in certain Indicators, when arranged in a particular way on the "Trade Navigator"© platform, are the best Indicator of all in spotting incipient Reversals of Trend; and

(2) *"Unorthodox"* Japanese Candlestick Trend-Reversal Warning Patterns carry much of the "DNA" of their parents, and are likewise excellent predictors of an

imminent change of Trend. Candelaabra is *beyond Candlesticks* and *beyond Elliott Wave.*

"Candelaabra" is not numbers-based. You do not need a calculator. "Candelaabra" does not use graphs or "Point and Figure." It displays *Pictures.* This is "Pattern Recognition 101." Your eye does the work!

"Candelaabra" does not displace "Candlesticks." ("Candlesticks" and the familiar "Candlestick" reversal warning patterns are essential ingredients of "Candelaabra"). Nor does "Candelaabra" displace or override the familiar "Western Indicators" or any other technical analysis system. Rather, it is *additive and complementary to all of them.* If a trader has a favorite system which he chooses to retain as his primary analytical tool, "Candelaabra" can be very useful to him as a *crosscheck.*

There are two main aspects of Candelaabra®: the "Extreme Readings" and the "Unorthodox Japanese Candlestick Reversal Warning Patterns."

A. *The Extreme Readings*

The key to the 'Extreme Readings" component of Candelaabra is the *particular selection of the Indicators, and their particular arrangement in the horizontal "Panes" of the Trade Navigator © platform.*

As usual, the Indicators are displayed as *lines.* They aren't straight lines; they're wavy lines, or "waves" (not to be confused with "Elliott Waves"). We are constantly searching for *contemporaneous extreme readings in Price and in the lines of the Indicators.* It is the *visual relationships between these extreme readings which comprise the Pictures that we are looking for.* When the relationship between the lines of two individual Indicators (or related groups of Indicators) is such that they are close together, we call that relationship a *"Crimp;"* (and if the two are especially close, we can also call it a *"Kiss.")* Conversely, when the relationship between the lines of two individual Indicators is such that they are spread far apart, we call that relationship a "*Blimp.*"

The secret here is that *extremes correct themselves;* so that when the lines of two individual Indicators are close together, they repel each other; and when they are spread far apart, they yearn to get closer to each other. There is continuous movement from "Crimp" toward "Blimp," and back again. There is a love-hate relationship between converging and diverging Indicator lines, which results in the formation of "Crimps" and "Blimps." So when we see a "Crimp" or a "Blimp" in full bloom, hopefully more than one of them at the same time, we *know* that there is going to be a change in the direction of Price – and, therefore, a change of trend.

This is not "rocket science." It's *Pictures!* Your eye recognizes the pictures instantly, for what they are – *Reversal signals!*

Let me show you how simple, easy, and obvious this is. Here's a Daily chart of Corn, as displayed on the "Chandelles" template in Trade Navigator©. (It could just as well have been a chart of a stock, or an Index, or a commodity, or Bonds, or Forex):

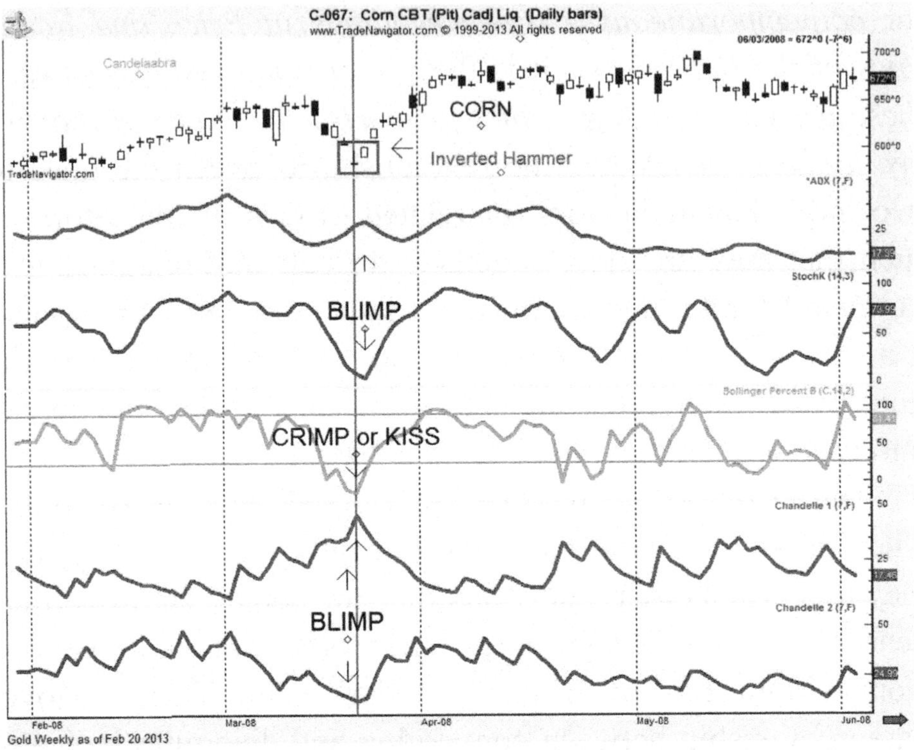

Corn

At the vertical line (depicting a single day), we see that the price of Corn has sharply declined into a Low, and that price action has formed a Candlestick "Inverted Hammer," which is a bullish Reversal Signal. (The "Inverted Hammer" would be clearly displayed on your "prices only" template in Trade Navigator©). We see that a wideness, a "Blimp," has formed between the lines of the top red and blue Indicators (ADX and Stoch K). We see that the green line (the Indicator "Bollinger Percent B") has spiked low. (The green line and Price will always roughly correlate with each other). Next, we see that the green line and the red line of the "Chandelle 1" Indicator are very close together, in a "Crimp;" and that they are SO close together that we can call it a "Kiss." And finally, (please look at the red and blue lines at the bottom of the chart) we see that the lines of Indicators "Chandelle 1" and "Chandelle 2" are spread widely apart, in a "Blimp."

So, what do we have here? Let's recap: Price is low; we have a "Candlestick" bullish reversal signal (the Inverted Hammer); we have a "Blimp" between ADX and Stoch K; we have a spike Low in the green line; we have a "Crimp" (which is so close as to be a "Kiss") between the green line and the red line which is "Chandelle 1;" and we have a "Blimp" between the red line of "Chandelle 1" and the blue line of "Chandelle 2."

This was a *perfect setup for a price rise. And that's exactly what happened!*

Do you see how easy, simple, and obvious this is? The combination of reversal signals jumps right up off the chart and hits your eye. This is "Pattern Recognition 101." Your eye does the work!

This works exactly the same in every time frame in every charted financial instrument.

B. *The 'Unorthodox" Japanese Candlestick Trend-Reversal Warning Patterns*

You will not find any reference to "Unorthodox" Japanese Candlesticks Trend-Reversal Warning Patterns in any standard "Japanese Candlestick" text. They are my discovery; this is a new field of inquiry, which I invented.

All but one of the "Unorthodox" Japanese Candle Trend-Reversal Warning Patterns that I have discovered to date are variations of either the Orthodox "Morning Star" or "Evening Star" Candlestick patterns.

The "Morning Star" pattern features a tall black candle and a tall white candle as "bookends," with a small candle (a "Star") situated between them, very low, at or near or below the "Real Bodies" of the tall black and the tall white. The "Morning Star" is a bullish pattern.

The "Nagoya Trader" is a variation on the "Morning Star." It is, therefore, an "Unorthodox" pattern. The "Nagoya Trader" features FOUR "Stars" between the tall black and the tall white. Like the "Morning Star," the "Nagoya Trader" is a bullish pattern. Here it is:

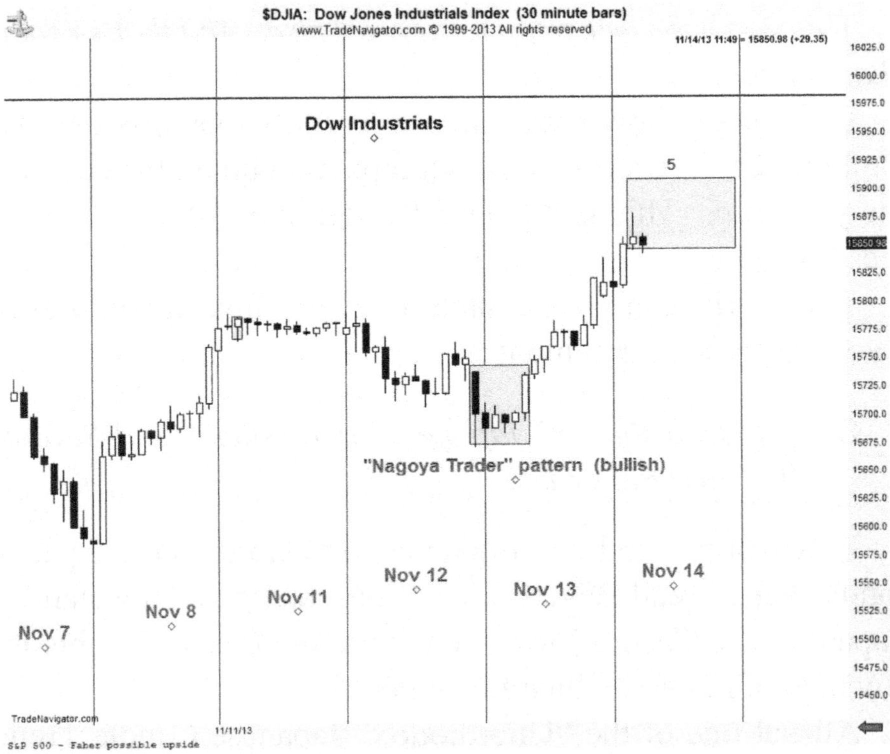

Nagoya Trader

You can see that this pattern's bullish promise was fulfilled. A traditional "Candlesticker" would not have recognized this as a Candlestick Trend-Reversal Warning Pattern, or at all.

Conversely, the "Osaka Clipper" Unorthodox Japanese Candlestick Trend-Reversal Warning Pattern is a variation of the bearish Orthodox "Evening Star," which features a single "Star" between the tall white and the tall black; and of course the "Osaka Clipper" is bearish too, just as its parent is bearish. The "Osaka Clipper" features TWO "Stars" in that location, at or near or above the tops of the "Real Bodies" of the tall white and the tall black. Here is the "Osaka Clipper:"

Osaka Clipper

You can readily see that the bearish "Osaka Clipper" fulfilled its promise. Note the reference to the two "Doji" Stars situated between the tops of the Real Bodies of the tall white and the tall black. A "Doji" bar is one in which the Opening price and the Closing price are the same, or very nearly so. When a "Doji" appears at the top of a long uptrend, it is considered bearish. Two Doji in a row at this location are considered to be very bearish. The appearance of the two Doji, back-to-back, enhanced the basic bearishness of the pattern. A traditional "Candlesticker" would not have recognized this "Unorthodox" pattern as a Trend-Reversal Warning Pattern, or at all.

The "Nagoya Trader" and the "Osaka Clipper" are only two of the many "Unorthodox" Japanese Candlestick Trend-Reversal Warning Patterns, both bullish and bearish, which have been discovered to date. More of them, new ones that we have never seen before, are being discovered from time to time. One characteristic of "Unorthodox" Candlestick patterns is that while this is a living, vibrant art in which new "Unorthodox" patterns are discovered regularly, the "Orthodox" patterns are fixed. New ones stopped being identified centuries ago. They are what they are.

You can use "Candelaabra" in order to enhance your trading profits by joining a new trend early, or to warn you to get out of an existing position before much damage is done when the trend turns against you.

....

To your investing and trading success!
Respectfully,
William Kurtz
CandleWave, LLC
info@CandleWave.com
906 Whippoorwill Drive, Palm Harbor FL 34683 USA
July 29, 2015

Introduction

The Rootstock of Candelaabra is Japanese Candlesticks

The Evolution of Japanese Candlesticks to Candelaabra

"Japanese Candlesticks" is a method of price presentation of charted financial vehicles such as commodities, bonds, stocks, stock indices, and foreign exchange. It was invented by a Japanese rice trader several hundred years ago in response to his desire to devise a trading advantage for himself. He tweaked the well-known "Open-High-Low-Close" price bar by simply "fattening-out" the price distance between the Open and the Close (that distance is called the "Real Body"). If the Close were lower than the Open in the time period represented by a price bar, he would manually fill-in the "Real Body" (thereby making it "Black"); but if the Close of that price bar were higher than the Open, he would leave the "Real Body" unfilled, or "white."

He found that this method of price presentation helped him to understand the psychology of the traders (as a group) against whom he was competing, by enabling him to identify incipient reversals of trend at an early stage and to take appropriate action with that special knowledge in hand. In the course of his investigation of his new price-display method, he discovered that some particular individual Candlestick price bar patterns were especially adept in forecasting trend reversals in certain environments; that they worked equally well and had the same meaning in all time frames (that is, within the "cocoon" of each pattern's individual time frame); and that *combinations* of certain Candlestick price bars were uncannily accurate in forecasting reversals of trend. He gave names to these talented individual price bars and multiple-price bar combinations – names such as the "Hammer," the "Shooting Star," the "Morning Star," and the "Dark Cloud Cover." Many of the names which he chose are reminiscent of their appearance in the natural world.

Steve Nison "brought Japanese Candlesticks to the Western world" several decades ago. The use and application of "Candlesticks" since that time have spread widely, and are gaining in general acceptance year by year. While the best use of "Candlesticks" involves substituting Candlestick price bar presentation in place of the old Open-High-Low-Close price presentation method, in all other respects Candlesticks is additive to the process, not taking away or supplanting anything. As "Candlesticks" is taught today, all of the "Western" Indicators are actively used.

The library of Candlestick instructional materials has grown quite large over the years. Numerous writers and speakers teach "Candlesticks," whether in seminars, in forums, through the use of DVD's, or otherwise. I am the only author and instructor who teaches "Candlesticks" differently from everyone else, in this respect: I teach that *every individual Candlestick price bar is either a "Classic Spinning Top" or a variation thereof.* (See my book entitled "Candlesticks For Brighties.")

"Candlesticks" Alone is an Incomplete Art

I have moved forward from "basic Candlesticks" by incorporating three additional knowledge sources: 1) Elliott Wave analysis; 2) my discovery that *contemporaneous extremes* in Price and in certain Indicators (as displayed on the "layer cake" panels of the "Trade Navigator©" platform) are often remarkably accurate predictors of a change in trend; and 3) my more recent discovery that *"Unorthodox"* Candlestick trend-reversal warning patterns carry the "DNA" of their "Orthodox" parents, and possess their trend-reversal capabilities.

Our understanding of "Candlesticks," plus these three enhancements thereof (Elliott Wave, extreme readings, and ***Unorthodox patterns) are "Candelaabra."***

"Candlesticks" alone is an incomplete art

"Candlesticks" is imperfect and incomplete. For example, while "Candlesticks" (even with "Western" Indicators added-in) is useful in identifying incipient reversals of trend, it cannot estimate the *price distance* of an expected move. In order to enhance the overall value of the "Candlesticks" approach, I added "Elliott Wave Analysis" to it. "Elliott Wave" is a method of ratio analysis based upon the number .618 and its reciprocal, 1.618, and their derivatives; and indirectly upon the "Fibonacci number series" 1,1,2,3,5,8,13,21,34,55,89 and on toward infinity – in which each number (after the first two) is the sum of the preceding two numbers; and also, after the first several numbers, the ratio between adjacent numbers is .618 or 1.618. "Elliott Wave" holds that a move which is in the direction of the trend will display a series of five waves, in "stairstep" or "sawtooth" fashion; while a move which is countertrend will display a series of three waves, likewise in "stairstep" or "sawtooth" fashion. In this way, I am able to overlay the *extent* and *probable ending-points* of price moves upon the "raw" Candlestick trend-reversal warning patterns.

This represented a "quantum jump" in my ability to forecast the fact and the probable extent of trend-reversal moves.

Still, I was not satisfied that the Indicators that I was using were "working hard enough" to help me spot incipient reversals of trend. For many years, I had been using Genesis Financial Technologies' "Trade Navigator"© platform, which features a series of horizontal "Panels" set one above the other like a layer cake, infinitely customizable by the operator. I had been experimenting with using and mixing various Indicators among the Panels; and quite by chance I discovered that if particular Indicators are arranged among the Panels in a special way, *contemporaneous extremes in Price and in the selected Indicators, especially in the presence of a strong Candlestick trend-reversal warning pattern, provide a very powerful forecast of an imminent trend reversal.* This carried "Candlesticks" one step closer to perfection.

I named my new system "Candelaabra."

Since then, "Candelaabra" has been expanded so as to include the new subject, "Unorthodox Candlestick Trend-Reversal Warning Patterns."

Examination of the Four Components of "Candelaabra"

"Candelaabra" consists of four components:

1. Classical "Japanese Candlesticks" (will not be taught here; the author assumes that the reader has read the author's companion book, "Candlesticks For Brighties" and perhaps other "Candlestick" instruction material as well (particularly the writings of Steve Nison), and understands at least the "basics" of "Japanese Candlesticks" charting.
2. Elliott Wave (will not be taught here, but reference to it will be made when the context requires it). The reader is encouraged to obtain and study "Elliott Wave Principle," by Frost and Prechter – the "Bible" of "Elliott Wave." Amazon has it. It's not expensive.
3. Real-life examples of contemporaneous extremes in Price and in certain Indicators (will be treated in this book).
4. A study of Unorthodox Japanese Candlestick Trend-Reversal Warning Patterns (will be treated in this book). This subject is my invention. It is taught nowhere else.

Contemporaneous Extremes

Candelaabra Component #3: Contemporaneous Extremes

The key to understanding the "Contemporaneous Extremes" in Price and in the Indicators lies in the *particular selection* of Indicators. and in their *particular arrangement within the horizontal "layer cake" "Panes" of the "Trade Navigator"* © *platform.*

As usual, the Indicators are displayed as wavy lines. When the relationship between the wavy lines of two Indicators (or between the wavy lines of *two groups of related Indicators)* is such that they are close together, we call that relationship a "Crimp;" and if the relationship is such that they are far apart, we call that relationship a "Blimp." There seems to be a "love-hate" relationship between two Indicators: when they are far apart, they want to move closer to each other; and when they are close, they want to move away from each other. *Extremes correct themselves,* whereupon Prices *move.* All of this is highly visual: the eye recognizes a "Blimp" or "Crimp" instantly. When we see a "Blimp" or a "Crimp" in full bloom (hopefully more than one of them at the same time), we *know* that there is going to be a change in direction of Price – and, therefore, in the direction of Trend.

This is not "rocket science." It's *Pictures.* Your eye instantly recognizes the Pictures for what they are – *Trend-Reversal Warning Signals.*

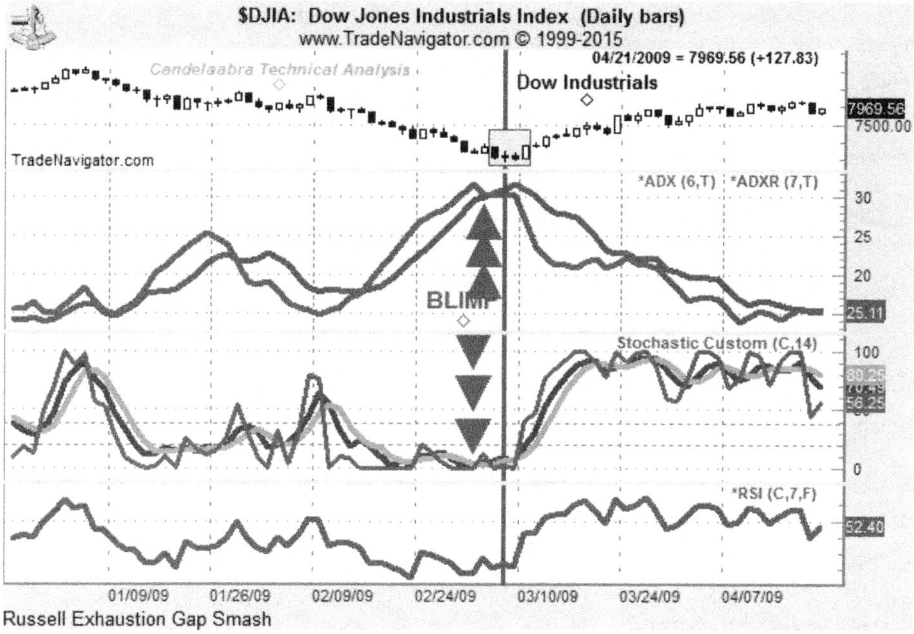

"Blimp" in DJIA

Here is a fine example of a "Blimp." Note that, at the same time, Prices were low, ADX was high, Stochastics were low, and RSI was low – all "Extremes." Note, also, the spread between the ADX and the Stochastics – the "Blimp." Your eye told you, instantly, that this was a perfect setup for a trend reversal, and that the reversal would involve a rise in prices. That is precisely what happened.

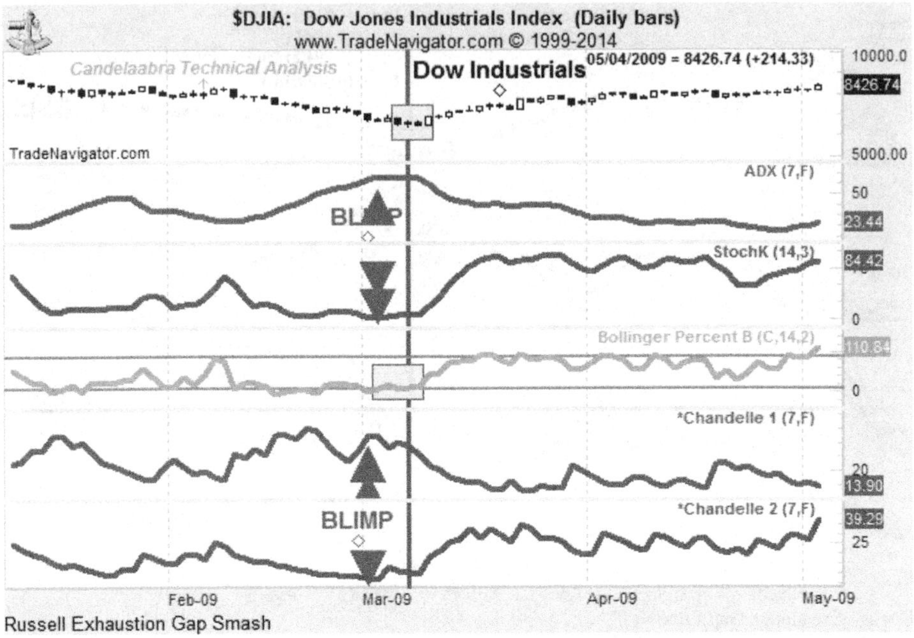

"Blimps" in DJIA

Here is a fine example of two "Blimps" on the same chart. This chart displays the ADX and the Stochastics Indicators, as does the first chart, above), and also the "Bollinger Percent B" (the wavy green line) and my favorite, the "Chandelle 1" and "Chandelle 2" pair, at the bottom of the chart. Note that (at the same time) Prices were low; there was a "Blimp" between ADX and the Stochastics; Bollinger Percent B was low; and there was a "Blimp" between the Indicators Chandelle 1 and Chandelle 2 – all of them being Extreme readings. All of this is instantly recognizable by the eye, on sight. Please note, also, that Prices rose, exactly as these patterns foretold.

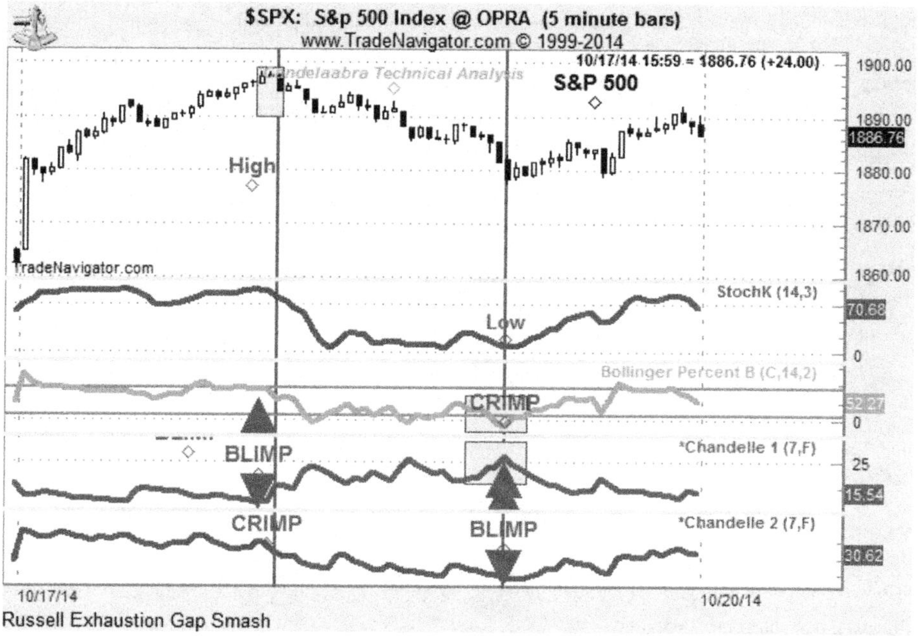

"Blimp and Crimp" in DJIA

This is a fine example of a "Blimp" and a "Crimp" occurring on the same chart. Prices were low; Stochastics was low; Bollinger Percent B was low, and there was a "Crimp" between Bollinger PerCent B and Chandelle 1; and there was a "Blimp" between Chandelle 1 and Chandelle 2. This was a perfect setup for a price rise – which is what happened.

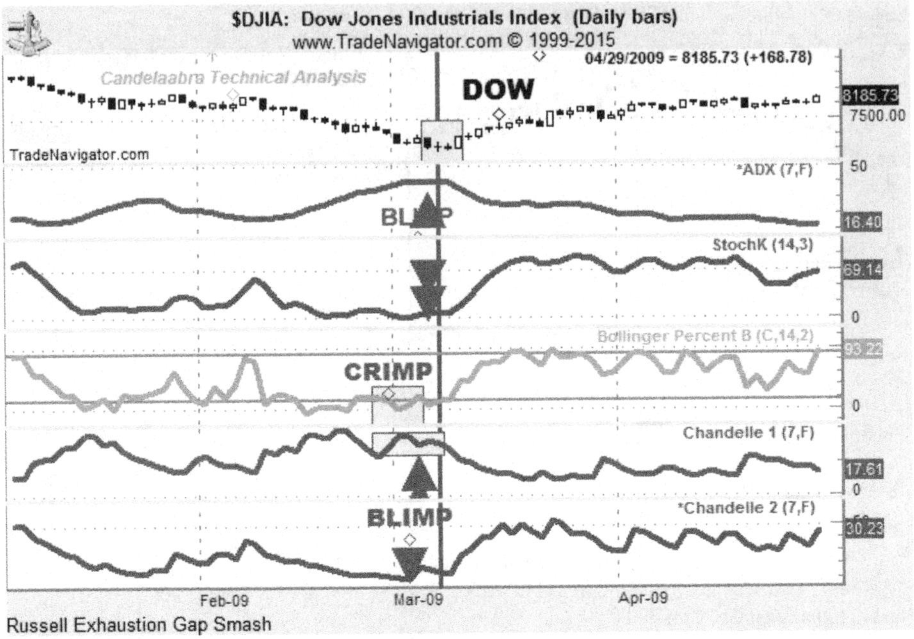

"Blimp and Crimp" in DJIA

I like this example (above) of "Blimps" and "Crimps" especially well. This chart depicts the Dow Industrials at the low in early March 2009, following the disastrous market selloff of 2008. Investor sentiment and Adviser sentiment were in the cellar. Well-known long-term investors averred that "the market has nowhere to go but down." We knew differently: We knew that the market was set up for a dramatic reversal of trend – to the upside – and we said so. Some of the reasons for our certitude lay in this chart. Please note the extreme readings: Prices were low; ADX was high while Stochastics were low – and there was a Blimp between them. Further Bollinger Percent B was low while Chandelle 1 was high, and there was a Crimp between them. Finally, there was a Blimp between

Chandelle 1 and Chandelle 2. This was a perfect setup for a reversal of trend – to the upside; and of course that is precisely what happened: This was the start of the Great Rally of 2009, which (as of this writing) has persisted for considerably more than six years – the greatest rally of all time.

Candelaabra presents trend-reversal setups such as these in pictorial form which the eye instantly recognizes. This is "Pattern Recognition 101." Your eye does the work!

Unorthodox Candlestick Trend-Reversal Warning Patterns

Candelaabra Component #4: Unorthodox Candlestick Trend-Reversal Warning Patterns

"Unorthodox" Japanese Candlestick Trend-Reversal Warning Patterns do not appear in the traditional "Japanese Candlestick" literature. They are my own discovery. This new field of knowledge is my own invention. It was I who first characterized them as "Unorthodox" patterns and began to assign names to them. As new ones appear from time to time, I continue to assign names to them.

Up until the time of publication of this book, all of the Unorthodox Japanese Candlestick Trend-Reversal Warning Patterns which have been discovered to date are variations of either (1) the classic "Morning Star" Japanese Candlestick Pattern, or (2) the classic "Evening Star" Japanese Candlestick Pattern, or (3) the classic "Bearish Engulfing" Japanese Candlestick Pattern.

How do they "vary" from their parents, the Classic patterns? Let us recall, for a moment, that the bullish "Morning Star" and the bearish "Evening Star" have one "Star" (a price bar featuring a very small Real Body) at, near, or below the upper or lower extremity of the Real Body of the tall black candle or of the tall white candle which completes the pattern. The "Unorthodox" "Morning Star" and "Evening Star" patterns will have *more than one "Star" in that location.* (In the case of the variations of the "Morning Star," the additional "Stars" will be situated at, near, or below the *lower* extremities of the Real Bodies of the tall black candle and of the tall white candle which "bookend" the "Stars." In the case of the variations of the "Evening Star," the additional "Stars" will be situated at, near, or *above* the *upper* extremities of the Real Bodies of the tall white candle and of the tall black candle which "bookend" the "Stars."

The "Morning Star" will appear at the bottom of a long, or substantial, price *decline.* The "Evening Star" will appear at the top of a long, or substantial, price *advance.*

Let us first examine the currently-known or anticipated "Unorthodox" patterns which are variations of the bullish *Morning* Star:

Variations of the "Morning Star"

1. The "Tokyo Express"

The "Tokyo Express" will have *two* "Stars" situated between the tall black candle and the tall white candle which "bookend" them. A fine example of the "Tokyo Express" arose in the Dow Industrials and in other Indices on March 10, 2009 upon the appearance of the tall white candle, which completed the pattern. This marked the start of the Great Rally of 2009-2015.

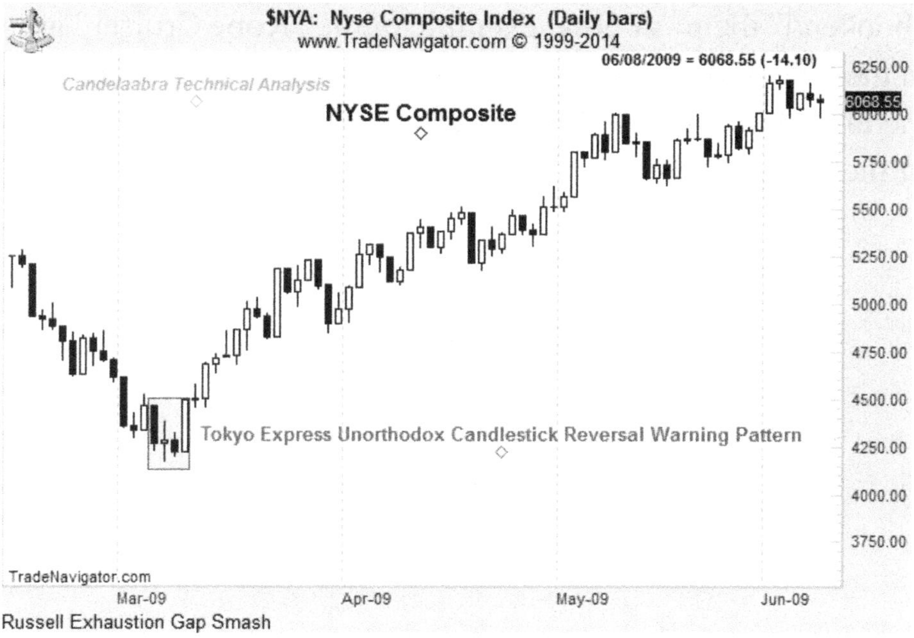

Tokyo Express

It seems reasonable to assume that the "Tokyo Express" is imbued with much of the "DNA" which infuses its parent, the "Morning Star."

This example of the "Tokyo Express" might also be deemed "Unorthodox" because the "Stars" are set too high from the bottoms of the tall black candle and the tall white candle. Note also that this particular pattern qualifies as a classic "Bullish Engulfing" pattern.

2. The "Kobe Cruiser"

The "Kobe Cruiser" will have *three* "Stars" situated between the tall black candle and the tall white candle which "bookend" them. A good example of the "Kobe Cruiser" arose in the Dow Industrials on July 13, 2009 upon the appearance of the tall white candle. This pattern marked the re-energization of the "Great Rally:"

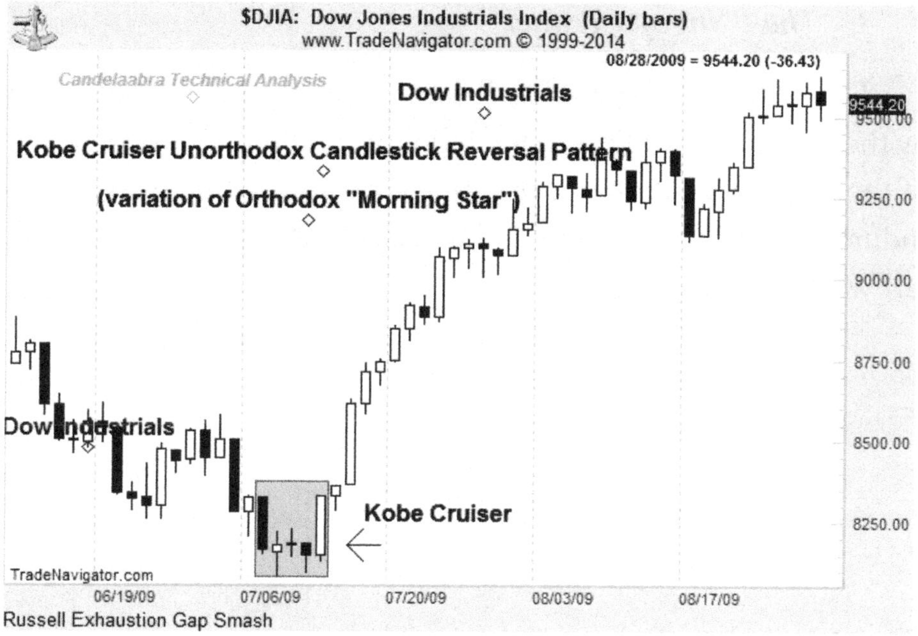

Kobe Cruiser

Having in mind the advance in the Dow Jones Industrial Index following the appearance of the "Kobe Cruiser," it seems reasonable to believe that this Unorthodox pattern carries much of the "DNA" of its parent, the "Morning Star."

This example also qualifies as an "Unorthodox" Candlestick pattern on the basis that the "Stars" are set too high from the bottoms of the tall black candle and the tall white candle.

It also qualifies as an Unorthodox Bullish Engulfing Pattern, because the Real Body of the tall white candle just misses "engulfing" the Real Body of the candle which precedes it.

"Candelaabra" does not concern itself with such niceties. It concentrates on examining the pattern in order to discern the mass psychology of the traders.

3. *The "Nagoya Trader"*

The "Nagoya Trader" will have *four* "Stars" "bookended" by the tall black candle and the tall white candle. A fine example of the "Nagoya Trader" arose on the 30-minute bar of the Dow Industrials on November 13, 2013 upon the appearance of the tall white candle.

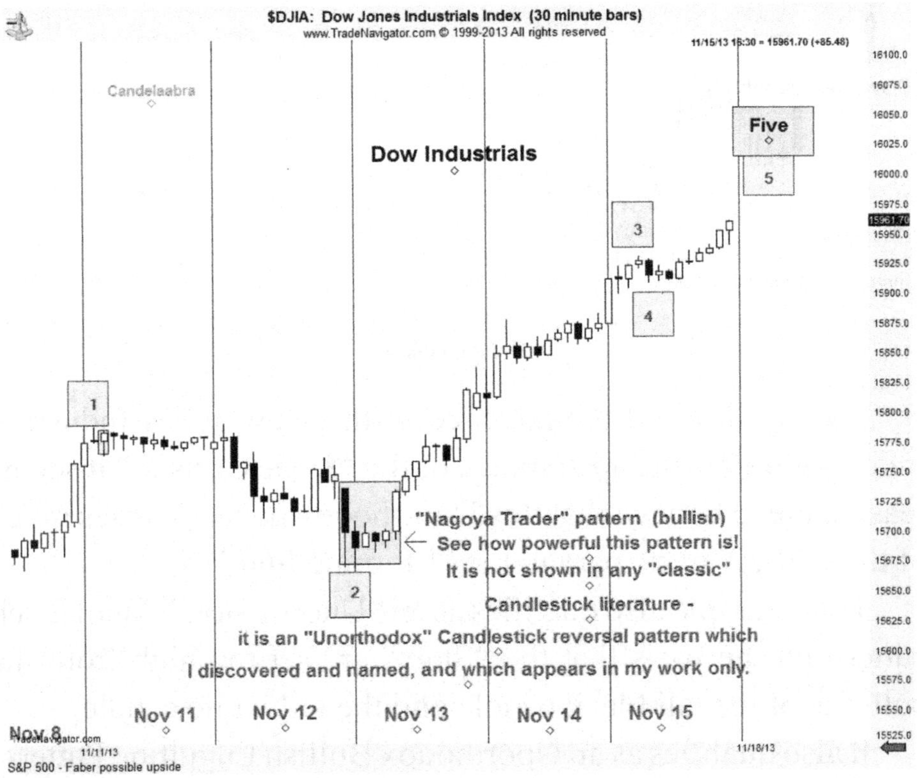

Nagoya Trader

As can readily be seen, the Dow Industrials advanced smartly after the appearance of the "Nagoya Trader" pattern. It seems reasonable to conclude that the "Nagoya Trader" is imbued with much of the "DNA" which infuses its parent, the "Morning Star."

This example might also be deemed to be an "Unorthodox" variation of the "Morning Star" on the grounds that the "Stars" are too large and that the tall white candle is too short.

4. The "Kyoto Scrambler"

The "Kyoto Scrambler" will have *five* "Stars." To date, I have not found a "real life" example of the "Kyoto Scrambler," but if one should appear, it will look something like this:

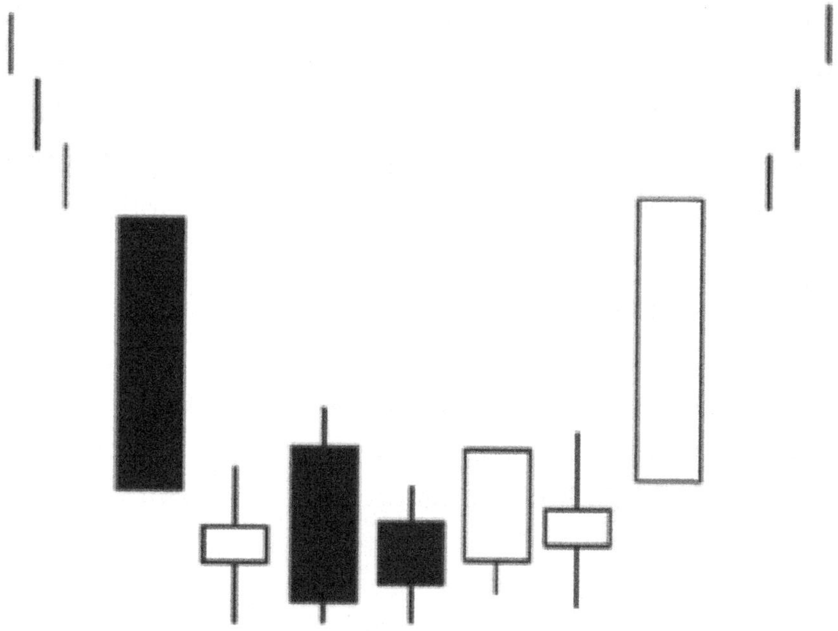

Kyoto Scrambler

If, following the appearance of the "Kyoto Scrambler," prices were to execute a pronounced rise, we could reasonably conclude that it is imbued with much of the "DNA" which infuses its parent, the "Morning Star."

It seems reasonable to assume that, over a course of time, other variations of the "Morning Star" will appear, featuring more than five "Stars" situated between the tall black candle and the tall white candle which serve as "bookends" of the pattern. I have not assigned names to those prospective variations of the "Morning Star."

However, several variations of the "Morning Star" have appeared, which are not "bookended" by single tall white and black candles. Nevertheless, they are legitimate Unorthodox variations of the classic bullish "Morning Star," and are testimony to my assertion that, in our ongoing search for "Unorthodox" Candlestick Trend-Reversal Warning Patterns, we ought to be governed by the spirit of flexibility of approach, with our eyes and brain always aware that nothing is cast in concrete – and that surprises await us if we will scan for Unorthodox patterns that do not "fit the mold" – *because there is no mold.*

With that in mind, let me show you several Unorthodox variations of the bullish "Morning Star" which are *not* "bookended" by a tall black candle and a tall white candle, one or both:

5. The "Morning Surprise" variation of the "Morning Star."

In this example, the three black candles were considered as one tall black candle, and the two white candles were considered as one tall white candle, thus equating them to the "bookend" effect that we see in the classic "Morning Star." This Unorthodox "Morning Surprise" pattern was considered bullish when it appeared, especially in the presence of the "Doji Hammer" as the single "Star." The pattern obviously fulfilled its bullish promise:

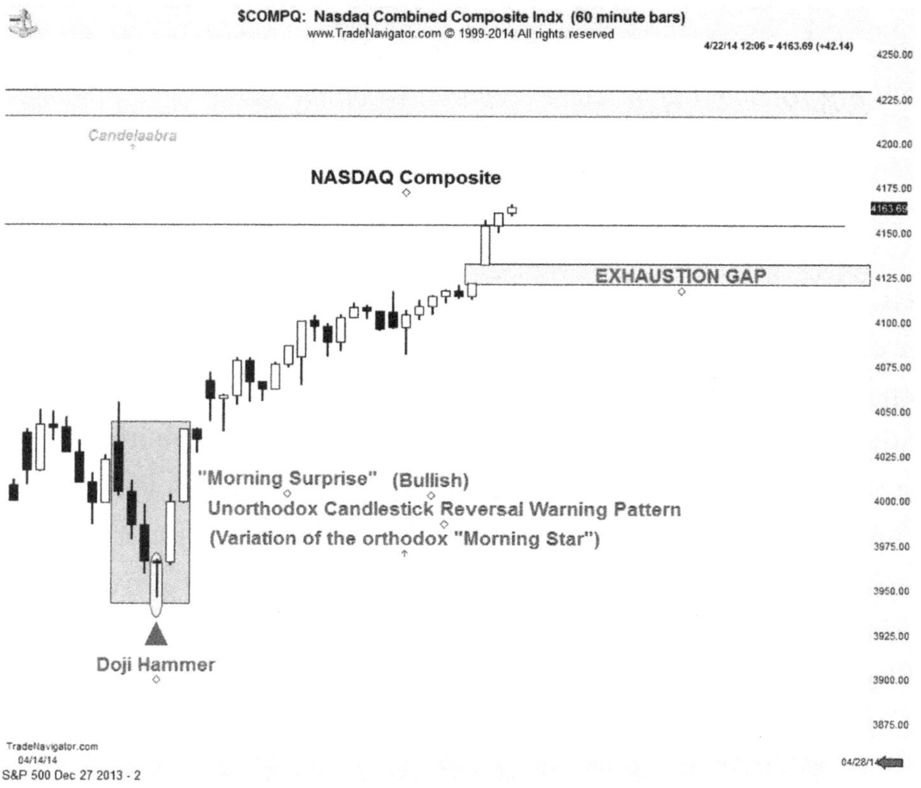

Morning Surprise

Did you spot the bullish opportunity here? When you saw the three black candles, the Doji, and then the two white candles which – together - more than equaled the height of the three black candles, what did that tell you about the psychology of the traders as a group? This pattern told me very clearly that there was a shift in traders' sentiment happening right before my eyes. You, too, will spot patterns such as this, if you will unlock your eyes and your brain from orthodox rigidity and learn to *search for and see unusual patterns which, although not "classic" or "orthodox" in nature, nevertheless clearly reveal the mass psychology of the traders. That's what we're looking for.*

6. The "Morning Glory" variation of the "Morning Star."

In this example, there is a small black candle and a single tall black candle which serve as the "left bookend," and the three white candles of roughly equivalent height serve as the other "bookend." The pattern featured two small "Stars," rather than only one, so the pattern can also be considered as a variation of the "Tokyo Express," and therefore is a variation of a variation. The bullish implications of the pattern were clearly fulfilled. This pattern would have been completely invisible to a viewer who is unskilled in the "Candelaabra" approach, even if he or she is knowledgeable in "Japanese Candlesticks." This is "beyond Candlesticks."

Morning Glory

7. *The "Morning Dew"* variation on the "Morning Star."

In this example, there are two tall black candles, two "Stars" (the second of which is a nearly perfect Doji, and two white candles topping out at nearly the combined height of the black candles. From the outset, the pattern as a whole appeared to be bullish. Since the pattern has two "Stars," it is a variation on the "Tokyo Express" as well as being a variation on the "Morning Star;" so it is a variation on a variation. This pattern would have been invisible to a viewer who is without knowledge of "Candelaabra" technical analysis.

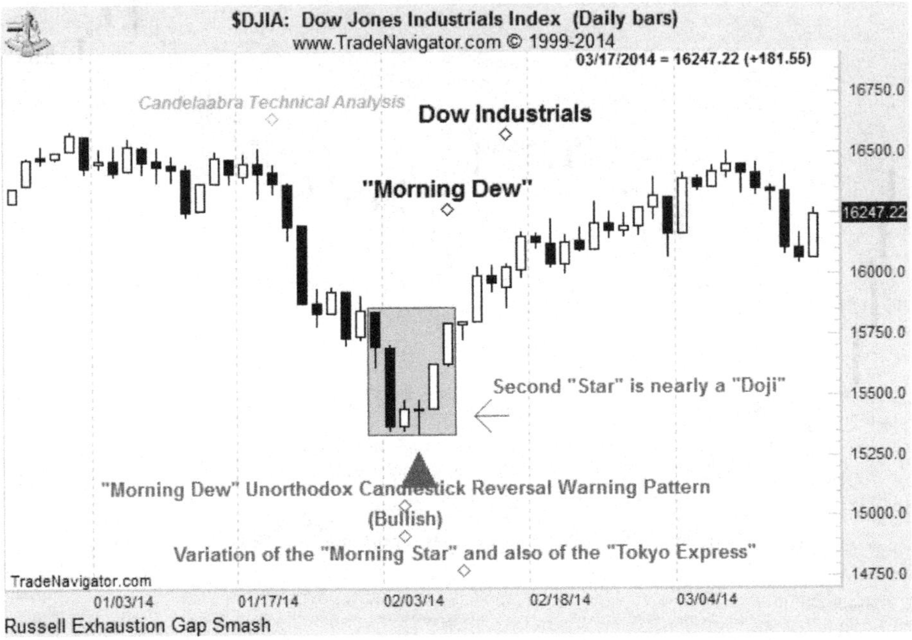

Morning Dew

In your search for "Orthodox" AND "Unorthodox" Candlestick Trend-Reversal Warning patterns, you may discover many more variations. The names of the patterns are not important. What *is* important is that you *recognize the aggregate psychology of the traders which the pattern reveals.*

Here is an example of the "open eyes" and "open mind" which we need to have, in our search for Unorthodox Trend-Reversal Warning Patterns:

8. *The "Double Black"* Variation of the *"Morning Star"*

In this example, the "left bookend" of the pattern is composed of *two* black candles which are treated as a single candle. The tall white candle which is the right "bookend" does not extend as low as it should. However, it was a vigorous candle, as the top of its Real Body extended above the tops of the black candles. Further, the "Star" was a "Doji," which is bullish. Overall, I count this pattern as a bullish Unorthodox variation of the "Morning Star."

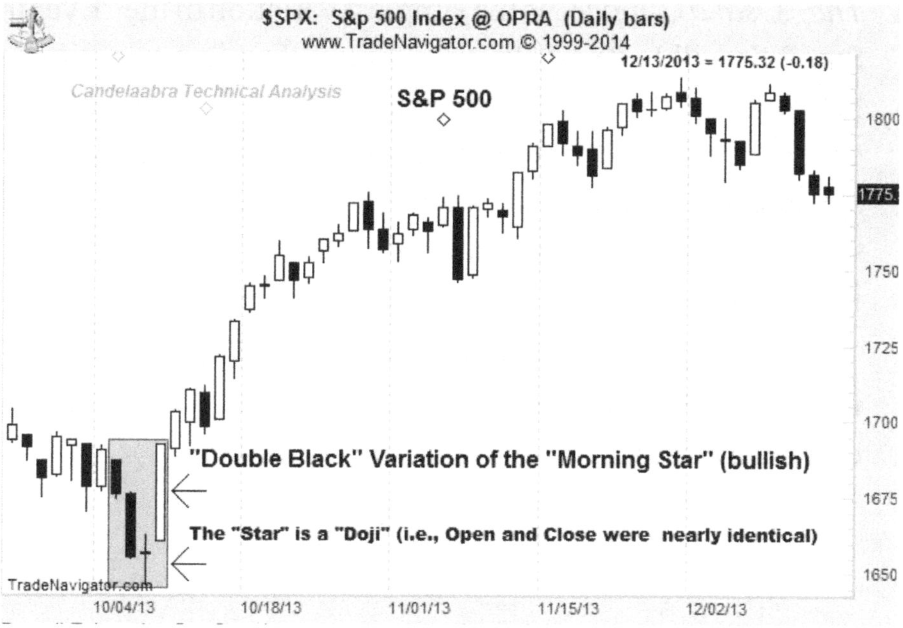

Double Black

"The proof is in the pudding" – prices rose smartly after the pattern appeared.

Variations of the "Evening Star"

B. Variations of the "Evening Star"

Now, switching from "bullish" mode to "bearish" mode, here are several examples of Unorthodox variations of the bearish "*Evening* Star" pattern:

1. *The "Osaka Clipper"* is the simplest variation of the "Evening Star." It will have *two* "Stars," rather than just one, situated between the "bookends" tall white candle and the tall black candle. Based upon the significant decline which followed its appearance, it seems reasonable to conclude that the "Osaka Clipper" is imbued with much of the bearish "DNA" which infuses its parent, the "Evening Star."

   This example is also "Unorthodox" in that the Real Body of the tall black candle as the right "bookend" does not extend quite high enough:

Osaka Clipper

Prices declined sharply after the pattern appeared.

2. *The "Sapporo Snowball"* will have *three* "Stars" situated between the "bookend" tall white candle and the tall black candle. The price decline which followed the appearance of this example, it seems reasonable to conclude that the "Sapporo Snowball" carries much of the "DNA" which propels its parent, the "Evening Star."

   This example is also "Unorthodox" in that the top of the Real Body of the tall white candle is too low; two of the "Stars" are too large and are set too low; and the Real Body of the tall black candle does not extend downward to match the Real Body of the tall black candle.

Sapporo Snowball

Even considering all of its deficiencies, it proved to be a strongly accurate predictor of a decline in prices.

3. *The "Yokohama Flyer"* will have *four* "Stars" situated between the "bookend" tall white candle and the tall black candle. The price decline which followed its appearance speaks to its bearish import. It seems reasonable to conclude that the "Sapporo Snowball" is infused with

much of the "DNA" which propels its parent, the "Evening Star:"

Yokohama Flyer

4. *The "Hokkaido Hustler"* will have *five* "Stars" situated at, near, or above the top of the Real Bodies of the "bookend" tall white candle and tall black candle. It is a variation of the "Evening Star."

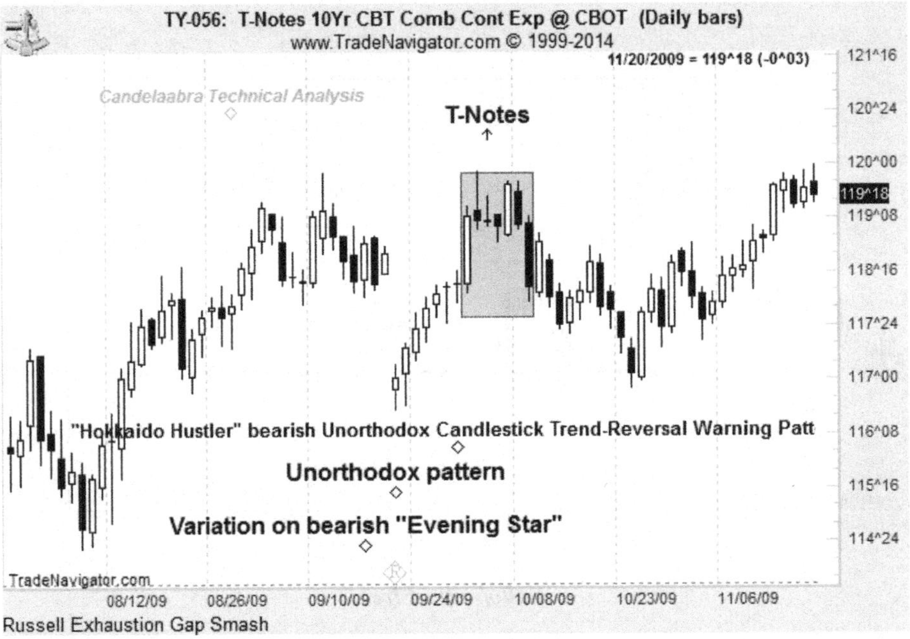

Hokkaido Hustler

It seems reasonable to conclude that the "Hokkaido Hustler" carries much of the "DNA" of its parent, the "Evening Star."

5. *The "Sendai Racer"* will have *six* "Stars" situated at, near, or above the top of the Real Bodies of the "bookend" tall white candle and the tall black candle. This example is also "Unorthodox" in that the top of the Real Body of the tall black candle is too low, and the tall white candle is too

short. However, that deficiency was overcome by the strong white candle which precedes the "bookend" white candle. Actually, the two tall white candles could be considered as a single white candle, in which case there would be different pattern entirely. In any case, the grouping of the candles discloses the bearish mass psychology of the traders.

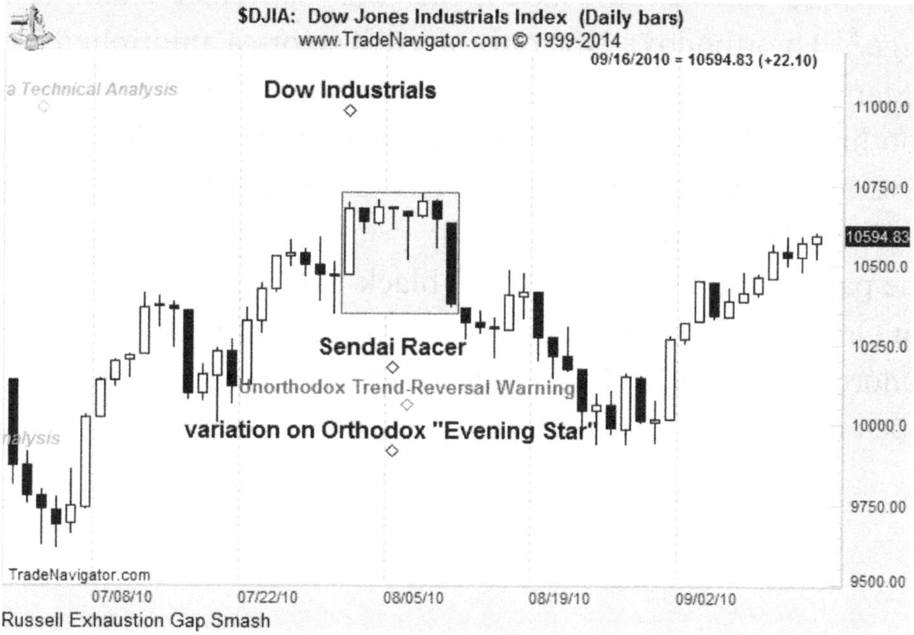

Sendai Racer

Prices declined after the appearance of the "Sendai Racer." It seems reasonable to conclude that it carries much of the "DNA" of its parent, the "Evening Star."

To date, I have not found an example of a seven-"Star" variation of the "Evening Star."

6. The *"Kanazawa Marauder"* sports *eight* "Stars" situated between the "bookending" tall white candle and tall black candle. This Unorthodox bearish Candlestick Trend-Reversal Warning Pattern was good for a 280 point decline. It seems reasonable to conclude that it carries much of the "DNA" of its parent, the "Evening Star."

There can be little doubt that this particular example is *highly* Unorthodox: Not only does it sport a multiplicity of "Stars," two of the "Stars" are outrageously large and are set too high. However, the "bookend" tall black candle is huge. Overall, the pattern discloses the bearish mass psychology of the traders. The proof is in the result: prices declined sharply after the pattern appeared. The large black "Star" just misses being an Orthodox Bearish Engulfing pattern. I would count it as an Unorthodox Bearish Engulfing Pattern. Keep open eyes and an open mind.

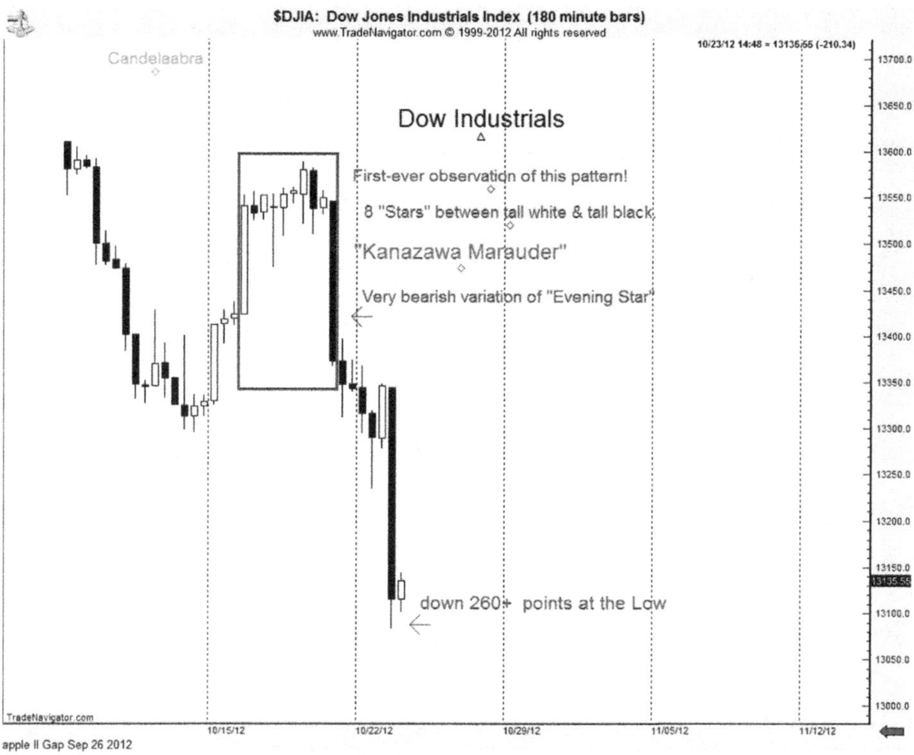

Kanazawa Marauder

7. The *"Kameyama Warrior"* features *eleven* "Stars" situated between the "bookending" tall white candle and the tall black candle. Following its appearance, the Dow Industrials declined more than 260 points. It seems reasonable to conclude that the "Kameyama Warrior" is infused with much of the "DNA" of its parent, the "Evening Star."

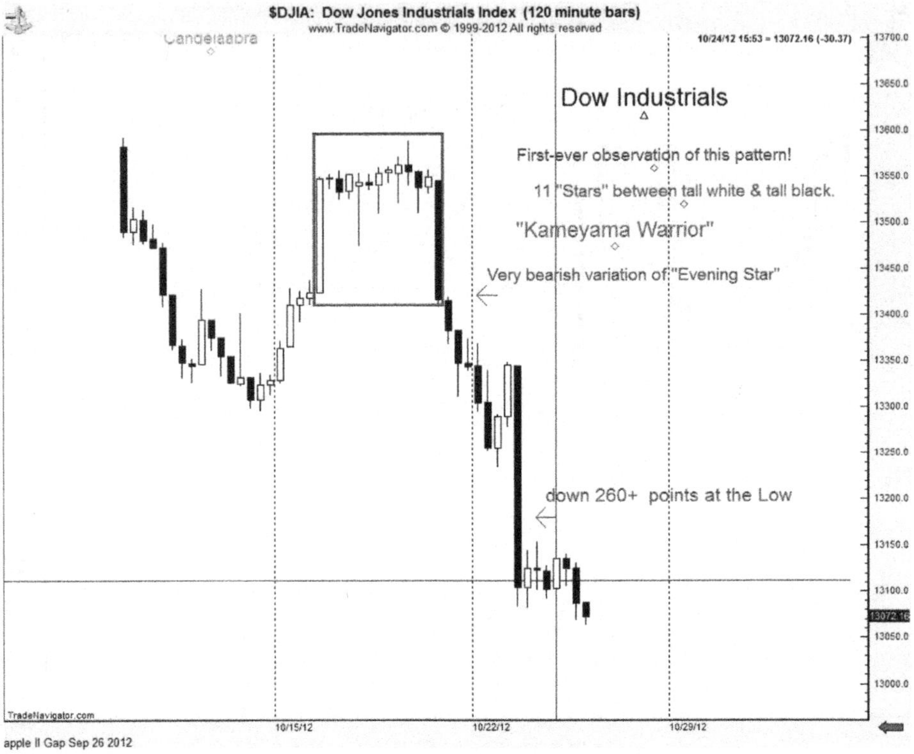

Kameyama Warrior

Variations of the "Bearish Engulfing Pattern"

C. Variations of the "Bearish Engulfing Pattern"

The traditional Candlestick literature holds that the Real Body of the black candle which "bookends" the right end of the Bearish Engulfing Pattern must fully engulf the Real Body(ies) of the candle(s) which precede it. In that view, there is no leeway for "near misses." I believe that is foolish. Strict, unbending allegiance to the rules can lead to substantial missed opportunities, while a little flexibility can lead to great "wins."

Here is the "*Evening Moonlight*" Unorthodox Bearish Engulfing Pattern. I count the two black candles which "bookend" the right side of the pattern a single tall black candle. By so doing, the Real Body of that "single black candle" "bearishly engulfs" the Real Bodies of 15 Candlestick price bars which preceded it. That is a very bearish pattern. Prices declined thereafter:

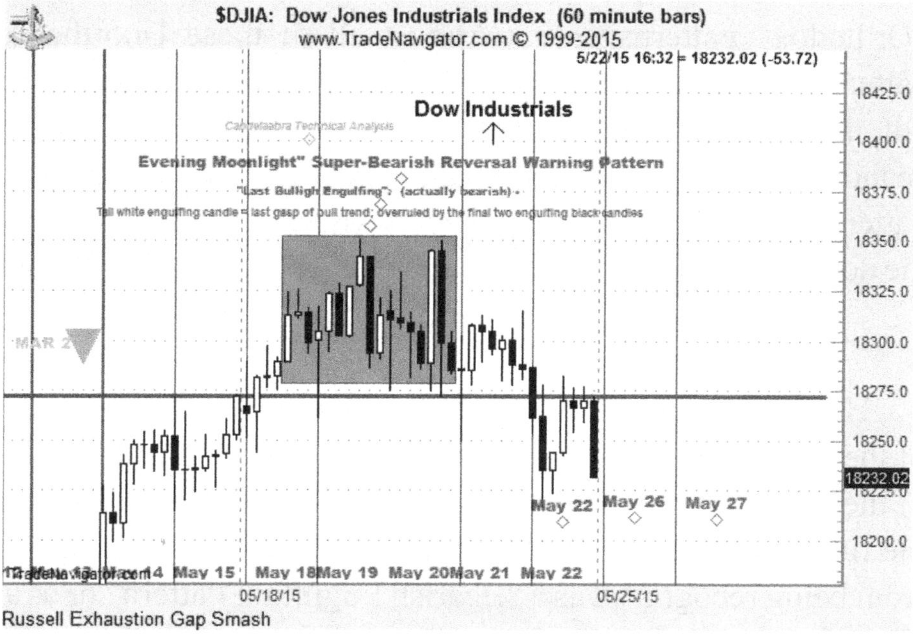

Evening Moonlight

The "Evening Moonlight" pattern revealed the bearish mass psychology of the traders.

Contrary to the standard "Candlesticks" literature, I do not believe in a hard and fast rule that the "Real Body" of the tall black candle which "caps the pattern" at the right end thereof must clearly engulf the "Real Bodies" of the Candlestick price bars which precede it. Rigidity in this instance can cause good trades to be missed, while a little flexibility can lead to good trades being taken.

It is obvious, I suggest, that Unorthodox Candlestick Trend-Reversal Warning Patterns do reveal the mass psychology of the traders to a greater degree than is the case when using "Orthodox" patterns only. Almost all of these Unorthodox patterns would be completely invisible to anyone who does not understand "Candelaabra" – not even the most skilled "candlesticker" would have seen them. The Unorthodox patterns reveal a world that we never knew existed. They open the door to new opportunities for investment, trading, and profit.

Highly Unorthodox "Bearish Engulfing Pattern"

Here is an example of a situation in which the "Real Body" of the tall black candle did not totally engulf the "Real Bodies" of the two price bars which preceded it. Strict interpretation of the rules would have precluded this arrangement of price bars from being recognized as a "Bearish Engulfing Pattern" or as an "Evening Star." However, those technical shortcomings were overpowered by the sheer obvious bearishness of the pattern. I would call this pattern an "Unorthodox Bearish Engulfing Pattern." The bearish mass psychology of the traders was clear, It would have been a shame to miss this Short-side trade on a technicality. "Close is good enough."

Bearish Engulfing Pattern

Conclusion

"Candelaabra" is beyond Elliott Wave and beyond Candlesticks. By reading the mass psychology of the traders and by maintaining an open eye and an open mind, profitable trading opportunities that otherwise would have been invisible come into view.

William G. Kurtz Jr.
Palm Harbor Florida, July 20, 2015

Appendix I – Closing the a-b-c Loop

Appendix

A. Mutual Reinforcement of Trend-Reversal Signals as between "Candlesticks" and "Elliott Wave"

and

B. "Closing the a-b-c Loop"

A. "Candelaabra"® is an "Open Discipline." By that I mean that it is always open to embracing new concepts which bear upon its features and capacities, including new discoveries - or explications of existing ones - that have to do with Japanese Candlesticks ("Candlesticks") or with "Elliott Wave."

The principles of "Elliott Wave" provide the best "compass," or "GPS," for determining where current prices are – historically, and in the general scheme of things at the present time. It is a system of ratio analysis, which provides the unique benefit of letting an investor or trader know when his analysis is wrong, sometimes even by a single tick. No other analytical system can do that. "Elliott Wave" is the best "barometer" that we have, for forecasting the general economy and for predicting where prices are likely to go next. "Elliott Wave" analysis provides the investor or trader with the most likely probability, and the next most likely. It delivers probabilities, not guarantees. "Elliott Wave's" delivery of price direction probability is the opposite of "guesswork" – i.e., "guesswork" in the sense of being lost and unsure, like finding yourself (figuratively) alone in a canoe in still air, somewhere in the middle of a fogbound lake without a compass or a GPS. That is where most investors and traders are, if they don't have "Elliott Wave" to guide them.

A basic discovery of R. N. Elliott (a true discovery, not an invention) is that prices which are moving in the direction of the operative trend move in five waves (numbered "1," "2," "3," "4," and "5"), in "sawtooth" fashion; and that price moves which are opposite to the direction of the operative trend move in three waves ("a," "b," and "c"), also in "sawtooth" fashion. "Elliott Wave" also posits that prices move in trends; that there are multiple "degrees" of trend which are operating on prices all the time; that prices move in patterns, not randomly; and that the patterns repeat and repeat - not necessarily exactly, but in formations that Robert Prechter of Elliott Wave International calls "robust fractals." (A nest of boxes of various sizes is an example of a "fractal:" the design of all of the boxes is identical; the only difference between them being size, or "degree," as Mr. Elliott described it). This discovery of a broadly predictable precision in the way the financial markets actually work is the opposite of a "random walk" and of the "Efficient Market Hypothesis."

Early in October 1987, Robert Prechter issued a "Sell Everything" notice to his clients. It was a prescient warning, for the "Crash of 1987" occurred several weeks later.

I had never read an explanation of what it was that Mr. Prechter saw in the charts early in October 1987 that prompted him to issue that "Sell Everything" warning, so I determined to go back into the Dow Industrials charts of that time in order to find out what that "prompt" was. (Perhaps this was a little akin to "reverse engineering.")

Here was the situation in the Dow Industrials in October 1987:

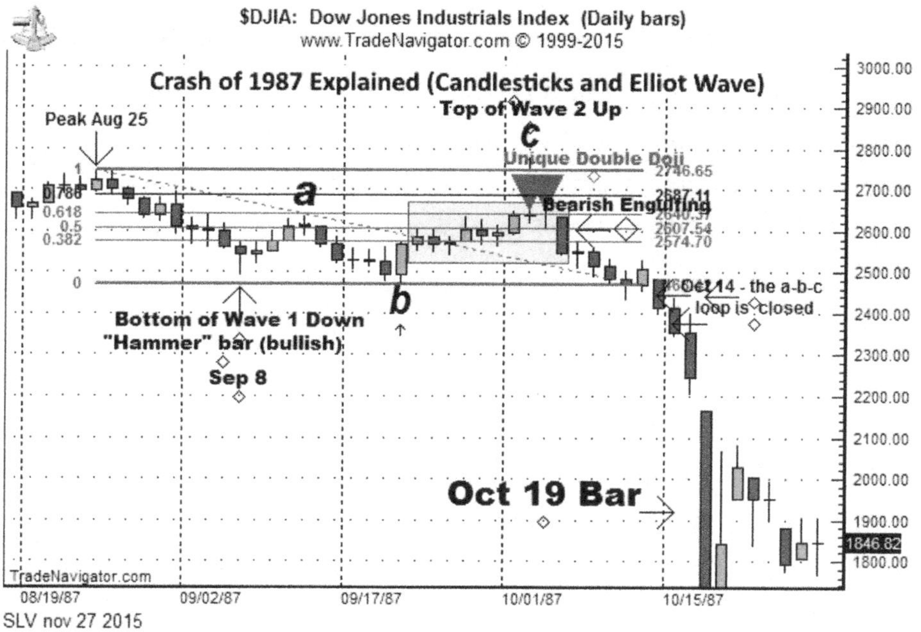

Crash of 1987 Double Doji

Prices had staged a long advance. Mr. Prechter probably had his eye out for a trend-reversal. Prices moved Down from a high level, and then made a turn Up, forming an identifiable bottom of a "Wave 1 Down" (in Elliott Wave terminology) in a possible new Downtrend, a switch from Up to Down. Prices then moved Up, Down, and Up again in "sawtooth" fashion, in what appeared to be an "a-b-c" upside partial retracement of "Wave 1 Down." (The top of the "c" wave, being the end of the upside putative partial correction, was also the top of "Wave 2 Up:" the 'a,' 'b,' and 'c' "sawtooth" corrective waves had "built" "Wave 2 Up." The bottom of "Wave 1 Down" was also the start-point of corrective "Wave 'a' Up."

From the top of corrective Wave 'c,' prices turned Down again. That turn probably was the trigger. Apparently, Mr. Prechter was satisfied that corrective waves 'a,' 'b,' and 'c' were complete, and that prices would now head smartly Down. This is "pure Elliott." (For the record, I have noted in my book "Candlesticks For Brighties" and in many other writings that the top of that 'c' wave was marked by the appearance of a "Unique Double Doji," two Doji side-by-side in which the Opens and the Closes of both Doji were nearly identical. A "Unique Double Doji" is a very rare and very bearish "Candlestick" pattern. Furthermore, the "Unique Double Doji" was followed by a "Candlestick" "Bearish Engulfing Pattern," in which the "Real Body" of a tall black Candlestick price bar "bearishly engulfed" the "Real Bodies" of several price bars which preceded it.

So, there was a "Candlestick" component of that wave 'c' topping pattern, too, not only an "Elliott Wave" component.

For confirmation that the trend had truly switched from Up to Down, Mr. Prechter could have waited until the Dow had fallen below both the bottom of "Wave 1 Down" (which also was the start-point of "Wave 'a' Up") AND below the bottom of "Wave 'b' Down." By so doing, the decline from the top of "Wave 'c' Up" (which was also the top of "Wave 2 Up") would have totally retraced ("gobbled up") ALL of the a-b-c upside partial correction, a definitive sign that the a-b-c correction had become complete, that it had now been extinguished, and that "Wave 3 Down" was then in motion.

I call an event such as that "Closing the a-b-c Loop."

At a time when the analyst's task is to determine whether the trend is changing (or has changed) from Up to Down, the Closing of an a-b-c Loop confirms the fact of a trend change from Up to Down. I expect that it works the same way when the trend is changing from Down to Up, but inversely.

(You can readily see that the Crash of 1987 did not "come out of the blue," as it is still remembered. Even without having recognized any of the bearish signals early in October, investors had multiple opportunities to exit positions before "Crash Day," October 19.)

(I've written elsewhere that the Crash of 1987 and the "Flash Crash" of May 2010 are "brothers under the skin." The only major difference between them is time compression in the case of the 2010 event. Each of them involved a slowly accelerating downhill glide in prices).

The next chart is an example of "Closing the a-b-c Loop" that occurred in January 2016. Prices had declined from a peak or mini-peak, had stopped falling, and then had turned Up, thereby forming an identifiable bottom of "Wave 1 (or 3)" Down. An upside (countertrend) partial correction of the previous decline then formed, as "Waves 'a'(Up), 'b' (Down), and 'c' (Up) "built" "Wave 2 (or 4)" (Up). From the top of "Wave 'c,'" prices declined past the bottom of "Wave 1" (Down) (which was also the start-point of "Wave 'a'" (Up) AND THEY ALSO declined past the bottom of "Wave 'b:'"

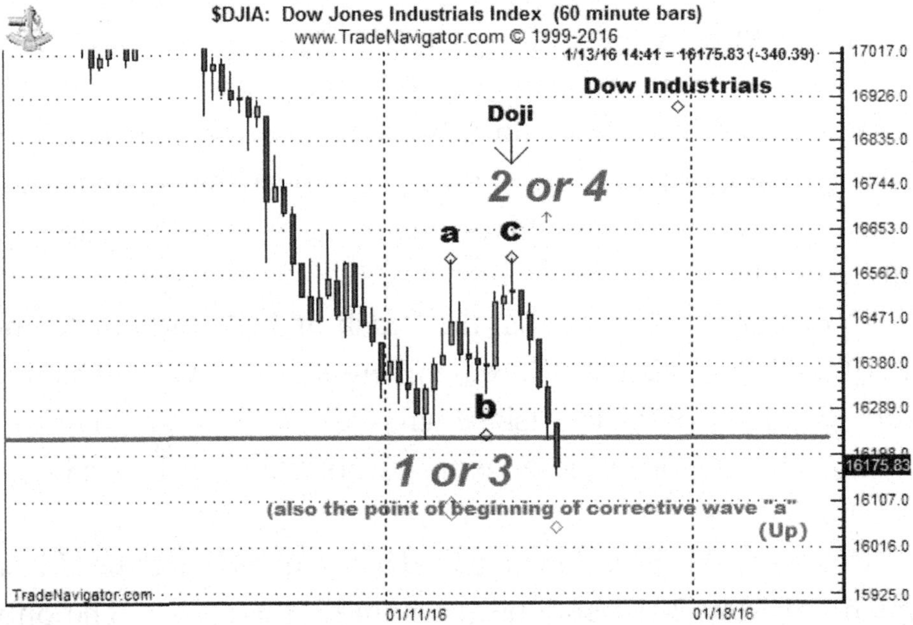

Closing the a-b-c Loop

The "a-b-c Loop" has been closed, because the decline from the top of "Wave 'c'" has retraced (i.e., "recaptured," or "gobbled up") ALL of "Waves 'a,' 'b,' and 'c.'" (It's a lot like "Pac-Man." Do you remember "Pac-Man?") This "gobble-up" confirms that the (heretofore) putative "a-b-c correction "had been real; that it has now been extinguished; that the operative trend is Down - and that it has been Down, all along; and that lower prices are expected.

Note also that the "Candlestick" price bar at the top of the 'c' wave was a "Doji," in which the Open and the Close were nearly the same. When a Doji appears at the top of a sustained price rise, it is a bearish signal.

Concurrent "Candlestick" Trend-Reversal Patterns
at the Shared Tops of "Elliott Fifth Waves"
at Multiple Degrees of Trend

"Elliott Wave" Theory posits that prices which are moving in the direction of the trend move in five waves, in "sawtooth" fashion. In a rising trend, those five moves would be 1 (Up), 2 (Down), 3 (Up), 4 (Down), 5 (Up). There are only three hard-and-fast Rules in "Elliott Wave:" (1) Wave 2 can never surpass the beginning point of Wave 1; (2) Wave 4 can never invade the price territory of Wave 1; (3) of Waves 1, 2, and 3, Wave 3 can never be the shortest wave (in terms of price distance covered) (Time distance is irrelevant). So, if you label a pattern in a way that violates any of these three rules, your labeling is wrong, and you would need to start over.

This Quarterly chart of Apple (below) displays a classic, well-formed "Elliott Wave" five-wave 1-2-3-4-5 pattern that, in the Spring of 2015, appeared to be approaching its zenith. The Candlestick price bar for the April-May-June 2015 Quarter (i.e., the Second Quarter) displayed a new High at 132.09 during the early course of its development, which would have caught the eye of an aware observer (but he most likely would have noticed that High sooner, on shorter-time-range charts). Apple closed the Second Quarter at 123.66. The Candlestick price bar for the Second Quarter was a "Doji Shooting Star," which is a bearish signal; and the Candlestick price bars for the First Quarter, the Second Quarter, and the Third Quarter (together) formed an "Unorthodox Candlestick Evening Star" (an imperfectly-formed "Evening Star"), which is a bearish signal, too:

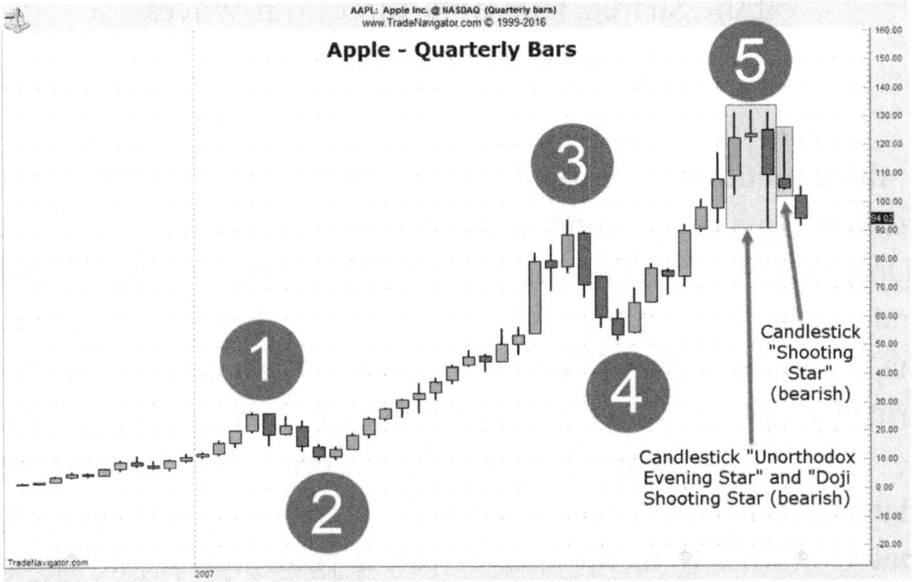

Apple – Quarterly Bars

So: The "Elliott Wave 5" and the "Candlestick" trend-reversal warning patterns cross-confirmed each other.

Now let's look at a continuation of the time-progression of Apple charts, from the Quarterly, down through the Monthly, the Weekly, and the Daily, to see how "Candlesticks" and "Elliott Wave" continued to cross-confirm each other (i.e., complemented each other):

Here (below) is a Monthly chart of Apple shares, also showing Spring 2015. It shows the same Elliott Wave 5 Peak (probably in multiple degrees of trend now) as the Quarterly chart shows, but the Candlestick price bar identifies the Peak price as having occurred in April. That price bar is a "Doji Shooting Star," which is doubly bearish. The emergence of that pattern would have been enough to claim the attention of a "Candlesticker," but there was more: the Candlestick price bars for the months of May and June form a Candlestick "Bearish Engulfing Pattern." The six Monthly bars at the top of the rise are, arguably, an "Unorthodox Variation of an Evening Star" – also a bearish sign. An astute observer might have noticed the possible emergence of a Triple Top.

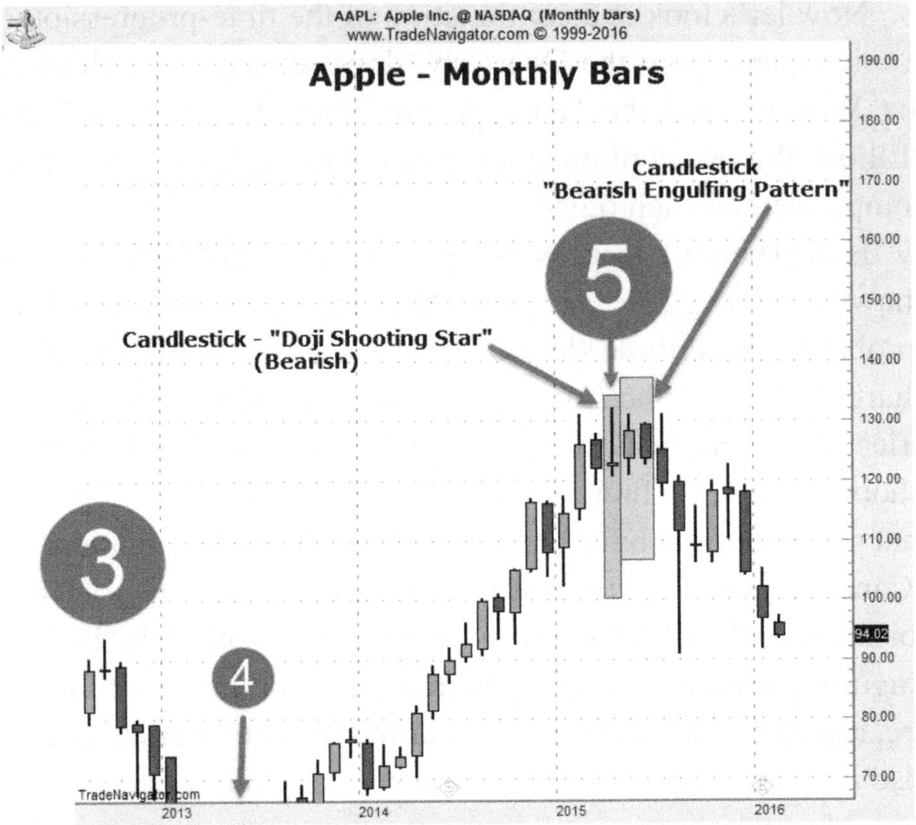

Apple – Monthly Bars

The cross-confirmation of a Top and probable Reversal of Trend continued, as between "Elliott Fifth Wave" and Candlestick trend-reversal warning patterns.

Continuing along, now let us look at a Spring 2015 Weekly chart of Apple. "Elliott Fifth Waves" at multiple degrees of trend are piling up. A Candlestick bearish "Dark Cloud Cover" and a "Bearish Engulfing Pattern" appear, confirming the growing aggregation of "Elliott Fifth Waves." The possibility of a Triple Top becomes more apparent.

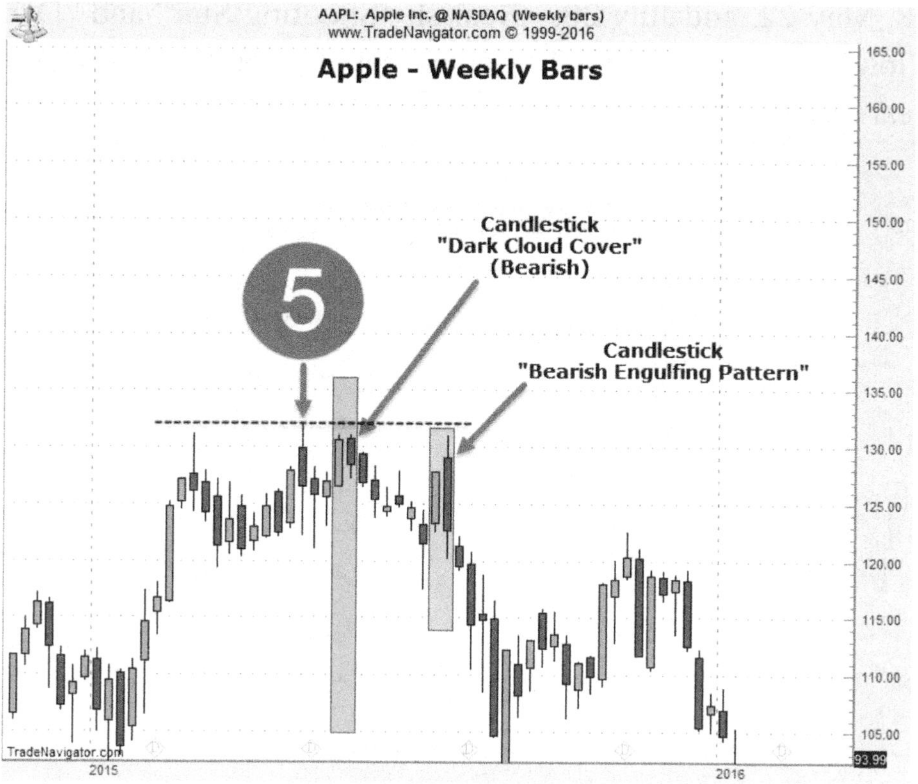

Apple – Weekly Bars

And now for the Daily chart of Apple, zeroing in on this topping process. Another "Elliott Fifth Wave" at a still-lesser degree of trend probably has been added to the Fifth Wave pack. The Triple Top has become clear. A Triple Top is a bearish signal. (I am not aware of any writing by any other author, describing a "Triple Top" in Apple shares).

It has also become clear that the actual Top occurred on April 28 at 132.09, not on May 22. We see three Bearish Engulfing Patterns in this "rolling topping process," on April

28, May 22, and July 20. Bearish "Shooting Star" and "Dark Cloud Cover" appear. The entire topping process projects a bearish cast:

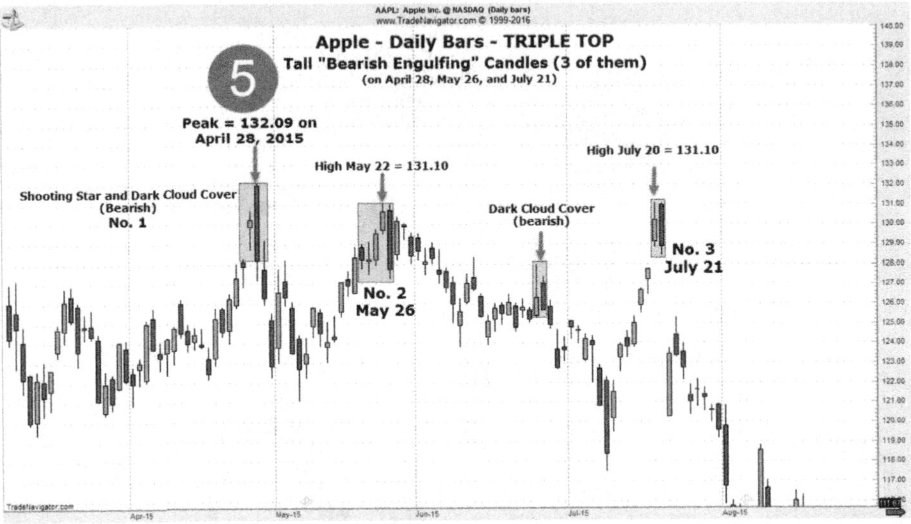

Apple – Daily Bars

The cross-confirmation of "Elliott Wave" trend-reversal warning signals and "Candlestick" trend-reversal warning signals portrayed an extremely bearish picture – a dire warning that the price of Apple shares had posted a major peak, and that the likely immediate and foreseeable course of their prices was Down. Subsequent price experience has borne out that prediction.

B. "Closing the a-b-c Loop:" The "a-b-c Loop" in Apple charts

This next chart is a Weekly chart of Apple, displayed differently from the one you've seen above. It demonstrates an "a-b-c Loop" that has not quite closed. As we've noted above, the price of Apple shares peaked and reversed trend from Up to Down in April 2015. Prices then fell to a "Wave 1" (Down) Low; partially retraced that decline in "Wave 2" (Up); and fell again to a new Low in a powerhouse "Wave 3" (Down). At that point, prices began to build an "a-b-c" upside partial correction of the "Wave 3" decline. The Low of "Wave 3" (Down) was also the start-point of corrective "Wave 'a'" (Up). When corrective "Wave 'a'" (Up) became complete, "Wave 'b'" (Down) followed, and then "Wave 'c'" (Up). At the top of "Wave 'c'" (Up), the "a-b-c" correction had carried prices as high as they would go. Note how the 'a,' 'b,' and 'c' Waves "built" corrective "Wave 4" (Up).

From the top of Wave 'c' (which was also the top of "Wave 4" (Up), prices have declined in "Wave "5" (Down), which is in motion and well-advanced now, and which will take prices below the Low of Wave "3." As prices decline in this "Wave "5" (Down), bits and pieces of the corrective waves 'a,' 'b,' and 'c' are being chipped away, or "recaptured" or "gobbled up," Pac-Man style. You may ask, "When will those Waves 'a,' 'b,' and 'c' have been completely 'gobbled up,' so that we can aver with total confidence that the correction is over with and that prices are certainly headed lower?" Answer: "When prices decline below the start-point of corrective "Wave 'a'" (Up) AND ALSO when they decline below the Low of corrective wave 'b.' When both of those events will have occurred, ALL of corrective waves 'a,' 'b,' and 'c' will have been "gobbled up." The correction will then be dead. The a-b-c Loop will have been closed. And that's a bearish sign.

This chart of Apple shares displays the incipient "Closing of the a-b-c Loop." It hasn't happened yet, but I believe that it will.

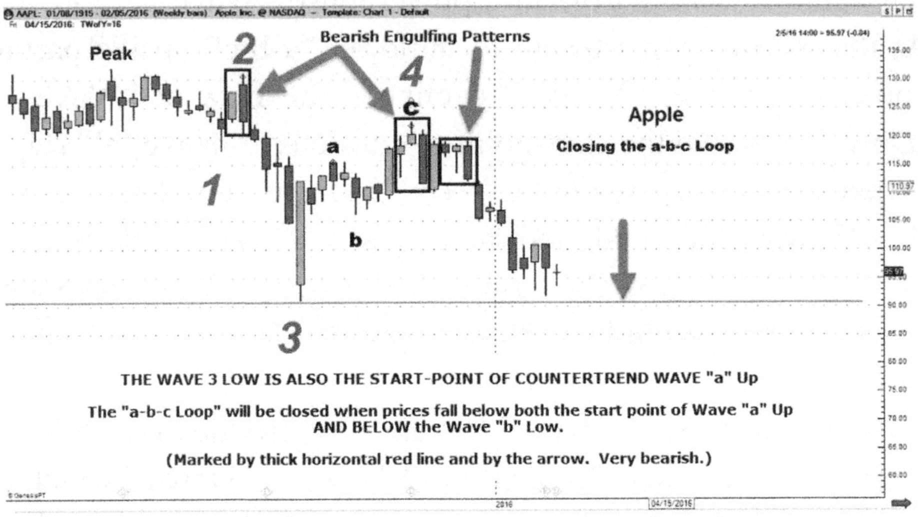

Apple – Bearish Engulfing Pattern

Prices peaked and reversed course at the shared top of "Wave 'c'" (Up) and of "Wave 4" (Up). The process of "closing the a-b-c Loop" began right there. Prices have already eclipsed the "Wave 'b'" Low, and are very close to eclipsing the start-point of "Wave 'a;'"; in other words, the first criterion for "closing the a-b-c Loop" has already been met; and meeting the second criterion (i.e., prices falling below the start-point of "Wave 'a'" (Up)), is within sight. The "a-b-c Loop" will then have been closed; and it will be a very bearish signal.

Please also note that the Candlestick price bar at the very top of the "shared top" was a weak Candlestick "Shooting Star" (bearish), and that the two tall red Candlesticks near the "shared top" formed "Bearish Engulfing Patterns" with the two price bars that preceded them, in each case.

I would not argue against an observation that, in this example, waiting for confirmation of the closing of the a-b-c Loop would have been far too long to delay before exiting a Long position in Apple; that the evidence was strong enough at or just after the "shared top" of "Wave 'c'/Wave 4" to warrant exiting Long positions at that time. This Weekly chart shows two "Candlestick" "Bearish Engulfing Patterns" at or near the shared top. (Indeed, this situation recalls Mr. Prechter's "Sell Everything" warning in early October 1987).

In this example, I also would not argue against an observation that too much time has been lost, and too much potential profit has been foresworn, by waiting for the closing of the a-b-c Loop before establishing a Short-side position. I would not argue against the proposition that there was sufficient notice at or just after the appearance of the "shared top" of "Wave 'c'/Wave 4" to warrant not only the exiting of Long positions but also the establishment of a Downside position or positions at that time. Opportunity is in the eye of the beholder.

So, this "Apple" example demonstrates yet another instance in which "Candlesticks analysis" and "Elliott Wave" analysis cross-confirmed and mutually reinforced the bearish outlook which each of them suggested.

"Candelaabra®" constantly searches for situations in which "Candlestick" analysis" and "Elliott Wave analysis" combine in offering each other mutual support, the result of the combination being a more certain forecast.

"Candelaabra" and "Elliott Wave" are natural partners. "Candelaabra®" understands and appreciates that, and builds upon it.

Appendix II - THE FOURTH COMPONENT OF "CANDELAABRA®" - UNORTHODOX CANDLESTICK TREND-REVERSAL WARNING PATTERNS

Appendix II

This Appendix II is intended as an Update, to consider three developments which have occurred since the date of the original preparation of "Reversal:" (1) new Highs in the price of Apple shares; (2) the "Double Low" in the Dow in January/February 2016 and the start of a new Uptrend at that time, which added 4400 points to the Dow through December 2016 and is still running as of the date of this writing; (3) the Low of November 4, 2016 and the "Jackrabbit" Unorthodox Candlestick Bullish Engulfing Pattern which followed on the next Monday, the day before Election Day, which added 2000 points to the Dow through December and is still running as of the date of this writing. (The election of Mr. Trump had nothing to do with it. The phrase "Trump Bump" is a misnomer),

Apple shares. The price of Apple shares has risen above its previous "fifth wave" High of April 2015. Question: Is this a new, higher "fifth wave" in the making, so as to require a re-labeling of past waves now? My response: Probably not. At the moment, I would rather call the rise from May 2016 a "b" upwave in a very large upside countertrend "a-b-c" correction, of which the "c" downwave (whenever it arrives) will drive prices far below their Low of May 2016. (See "Closing the a-b-c Loop" in Appendix I).

Contemporaneous Extreme readings in Price and in Indicators

The Lows of January 20 and February 11, 2016 (a "Double Low") were Lows of great significance. The upturn which began after the second Low marked the beginning of a new trend, this one being of "Intermediate" degree, which is roughly "half-way up the ladder" in terms of rank. Its life will consist of five waves of the one lesser degree of trend – up, down, up, down, up. It's working on its fifth (and final) wave now. This trend is dragging along with it the fifth (and final) waves of the successively next higher "degrees" of trend – the Primary, the Cycle, and the Supercycle; and it is also dragging the Grand Supercycle into its third wave peak. All of these peaks will occur at the same time. (All trends of various "degrees" operate side-by-side in the market at all times. The current market price of a charted financial instrument is the net result of all of that tugging and hauling). The oncoming contemporaneous fifth-wave peak of all degrees of trend through Supercycle, plus a third-wave peak at Grand Supercycle degree, has never happened before. Not ever. The bear market that will follow the unified peaking process will be cataclysmic. The 2009 Low in the Dow will be just a "mile post" on the way down.

Let me show you how the Extreme Readings in Price and in selected Indicators on January 20 and February 11, 2016 produced a powerful, unmistakable setup for an immediate price rise. (The Low in the Dow on January 20 was 15450.56; the February 11 Low in the Dow was 15503.01):

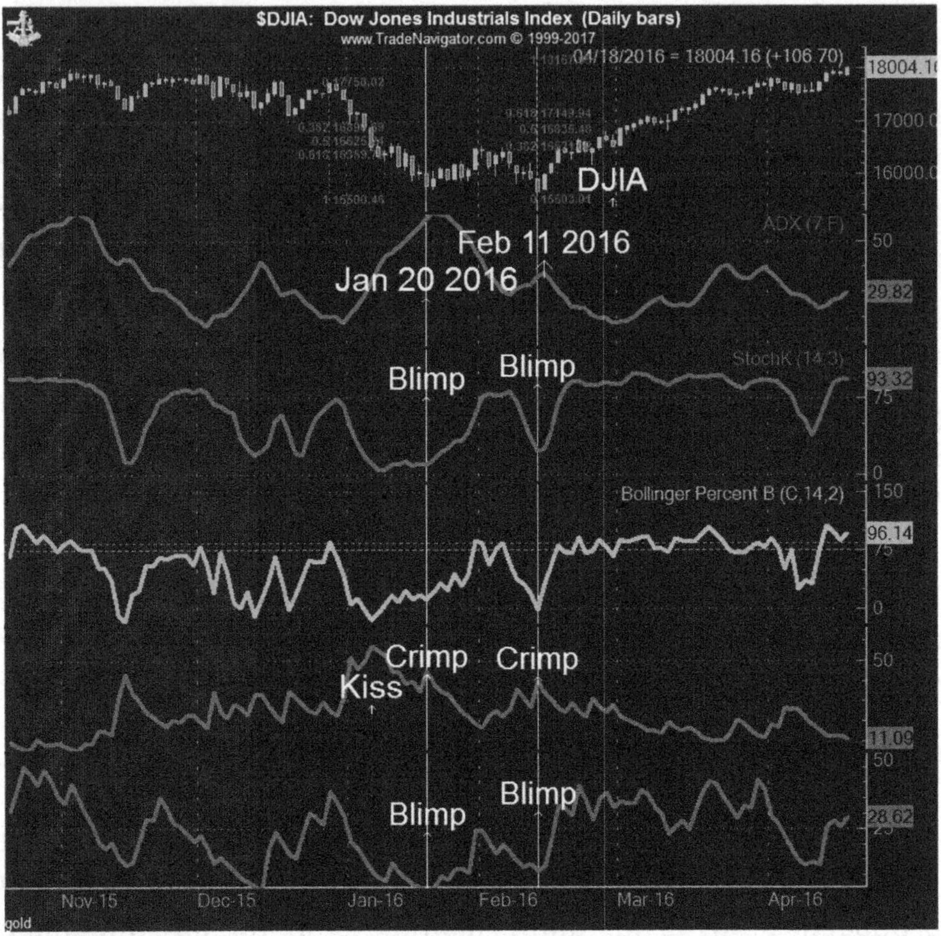

This chart reveals the powerful Reversal signals that are generated by a same-day comparison of Extreme readings in Price and in selected Indicators. This comparison is unique to "Candelaabra" and is not available anywhere else.

Let's look at January 20 first. Price was low; there was a "Blimp" (a wide space) between ADX (red line at the top) and Stochastics (the blue line beneath the red line); there was a modest “Crimp” (a narrowing) between Bollinger Percent B (the green line) and the red line below it (which is Chandelle 1) (but note the tight “Crimp,” or “Kiss,” a few days earlier); and there was a wide “Blimp” between Chandelle 1 and Chandelle 2 (the red and blue lines at the bottom of the chart).

All of these signals, together, constituted a strong warning of a probable price reversal to the upside.

The “clincher” was the “repeat performance” of Extremes in Price and in Indicators that occurred on February 11. Here again, we see that Price was low; there was a “Blimp” between ADX and Stochastics; the green line had dived deeper than it had on January 20, and there was a tighter “Crimp” between the green line and the red line below it, which is Chandelle 1. Note the large “Blimp” between Chandelle 1 and Chandelle 2 at the bottom of the chart.

By themselves, these Extreme readings of February 11 were a strong warning of a probable price reversal to the upside. In concert with the readings of January 20 (and of the “Kiss” a few days before that), the probability of a price reversal to the upside approached 100%. “The proof is in the pudding:” the Dow rose 4400 points from February 11 through December.

. . . .

The events of November 4 and 7, 2016

The Dow Industrials declined quite sharply into a Low on Friday, November 4.

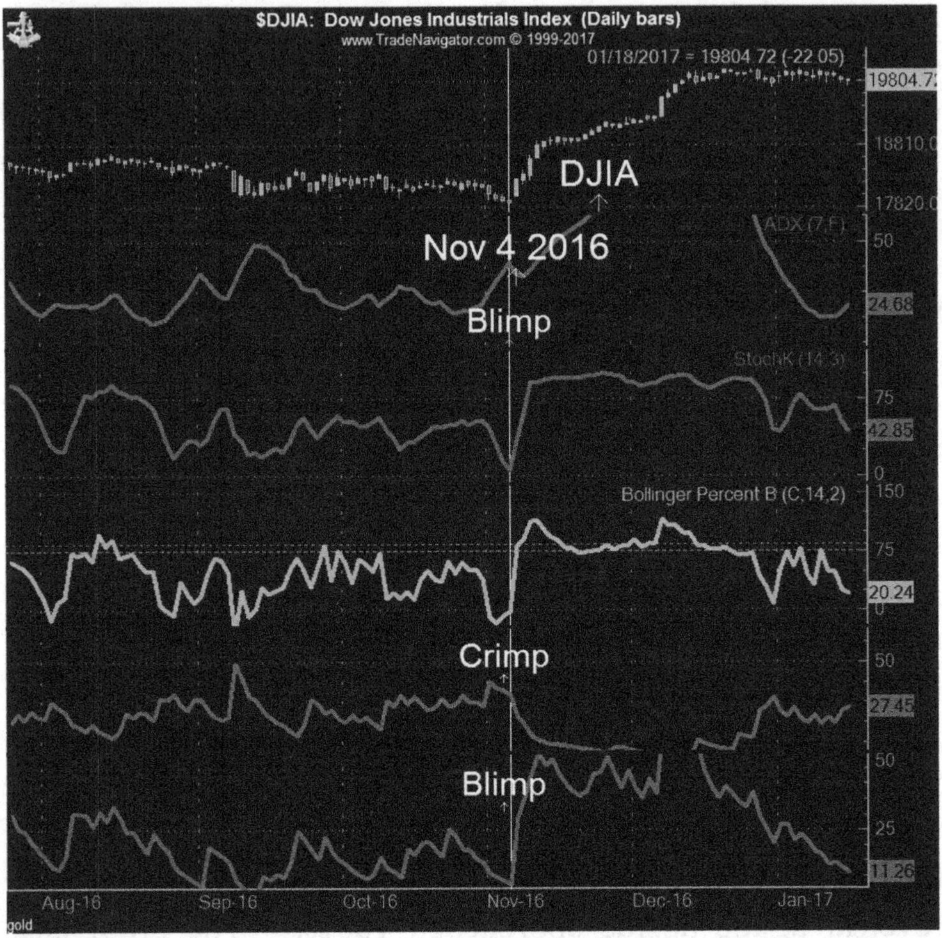

On the same day, a substantial "Blimp" (wide space) formed between ADX and the Stochastics (red and blue lines near the top of the chart). There was a substantial "Crimp" (tightness) between Bollinger Percent B (the green line) and Chandelle 1 the red line below it); and there was a wide "Blimp" between Chandelle 1 and Chandelle 2 (the red and blue lines at the bottom of the chart). This was a classic setup for a price reversal to the upside.

The reversal arrived on the following Monday, November 7, the day before Election Day, when prices gapped up on Open. Prices continued higher during the day, and closed higher on the day. Price action of the day formed an Unorthodox Candlestick Bullish Engulfing Pattern: the "Real Body" of the price bar of November 7 (including the opening gap, which is the "Unorthodox" part) "bullishly engulfed" the "Real Bodies" of the 18 price bars which preceded it.

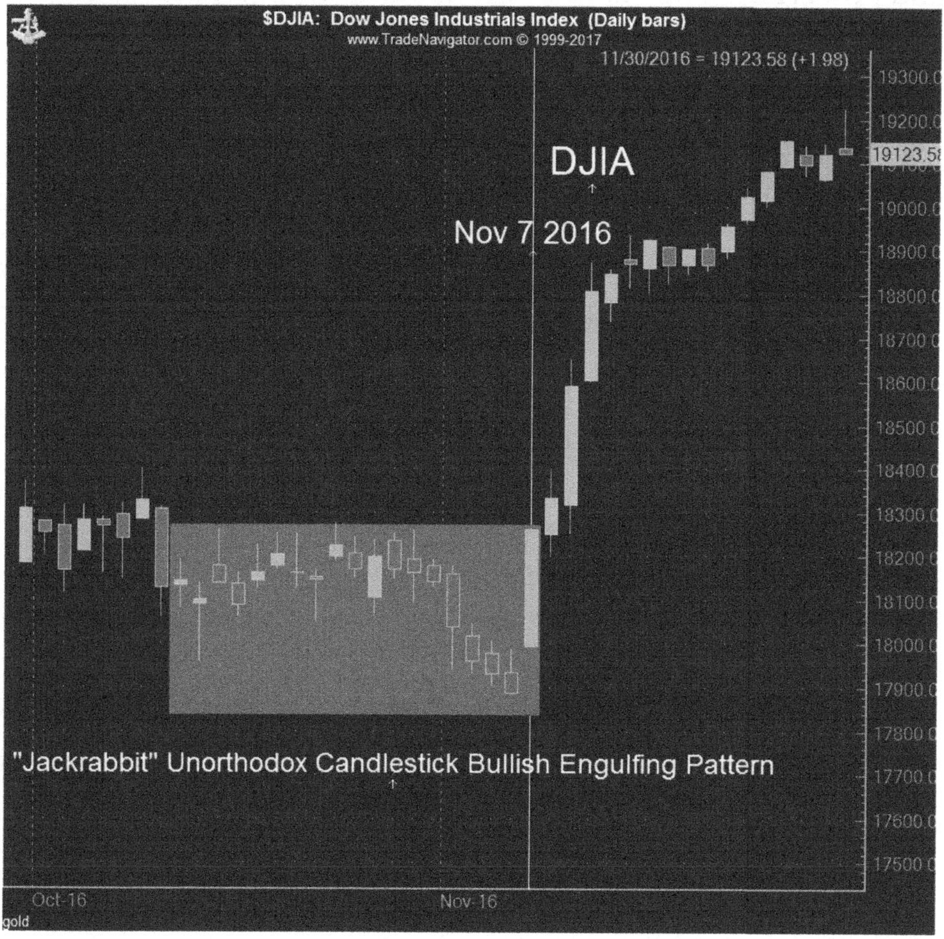

This was a powerfully bullish pattern. The turnabout marked the start of another trend, which carried the Dow 2000 points higher through December, and as of this writing it's still running.

The bottom line is this: Candelaabra's unique Reversal anticipation and spotting tools – "Contemporaneous Extremes in Price and in Indicators," and "Unorthodox Candlestick Trend-Reversal Warning Patterns" – are uncannily accurate and powerful. They are not available from any other source.

"The Money Is In The Reversal."

This is "Pattern Recognition 101."

Your eye does the work!

. . . .

Respectfully submitted.

William Kurtz
CandleWave, LLC
Palm Harbor, Florida 34683
Wkurtz1@verizon.net
February 12, 2017

Use of "Trade Navigator"© charts throughout this book is by the gracious courtesy of Genesis Financial Technologies, Inc., the owner of "Trade Navigator."©

Made in United States
Orlando, FL
04 November 2026

90207811R00046